I HATE BRETT FAVRE

The Brett Favre Fans Love to Hate

ROSS BERNSTEIN

TRIUMPH
BOOKS

ABOUT THE AUTHOR

Ross Bernstein is the bestselling author of more than 40 sports books and has appeared on thousands of local and national television and radio shows, including on CNN, ESPN, and NPR, as well as in the pages of the *Wall Street Journal*, *New York Times*, and *USA Today*. As a sought-after motivational speaker, Ross offers two programs. The first, "When it comes to team-building, leadership, and motivation…Do You Believe in Miracles?" ties into the inspirational legacy of the late Hall of Fame hockey coach Herb Brooks. To honor his friend and mentor, Ross speaks about the influence Brooks had on the world of sports and about the impact of the now-legendary "Miracle on Ice." Putting many of the life lessons and ideologies he learned from the fiery coach into a practical business application, his presentation aims to inspire others to follow their dreams and maybe, just maybe, even create their own miracles. The second, "What's Your Code?" ties into Ross' popular series of hockey, baseball, and football *Code* books that he has published with Triumph Books. Here Ross talks about the fine line between cheating and gamesmanship in sports as it pertains to ethics and accountability. There is an honor code in professional sports, a series of unwritten and unspoken rules, which allows the players to police themselves. If a player cheats, shows somebody up, takes shortcuts, or disrespects someone out on the ice, diamond, or gridiron—they will have to be held accountable or else be prepared to pay a severe price—and the same is true in business. Ross and his wife have one daughter and reside in the Twin Cities.

ACKNOWLEDGMENTS

I want to thank everyone who was kind enough to let me interview them for this book, all 100 or so of you. Regardless of where your quotes appear—on the "love" side or the "hate" side—it is all meant in good fun. Thanks for helping to celebrate the greatest rivalry in the NFL.

CONTENTS

Why I Love
to Hate
Brett Favre

IF YOU'VE OPENED THE BOOK TO THIS SIDE FIRST, you're probably not a big fan of Brett Favre. Welcome! Hey, I've been there. Trust me, I feel your pain. For 16 years the guy tortured me, too. I went from hating him to loving him, and you probably went from loving him to hating him. It's confusing. Who knows? We may all need a No. 4 12 step program to deal with our Favre-related flip-flopping issues when this is all said and done. Either way, in this half of the book I am going to dissect just why I, along with so many others, figuratively and literally, love to hate Brett Favre.

If you're from Wisconsin and you're a die-hard Pack fan, I feel for you. I really do. What Brett Favre did, by coming to Minnesota, is so wrong on so many different levels. I keep trying to find a good analogy, to compare it to on an apples-to-apples basis—like when Michael Jordan went to the Wizards, or Willie Mays went to the Mets, or Johnny Unitas went to the Chargers, or Joe Namath went to the

Rams, or Joe Montana went to the Chiefs, or even when Vince Lombardi went to the Redskins—but I can't put my finger on it. All of those players were legends in their own rights, and their departures from their hometowns were big deals, but nothing can really compare to Favre coming to Minnesota. Nothing. Well, maybe when Roger Clemens went from the Boston Red Sox to the New York Yankees, but that was after spending two seasons in Toronto. Even the hypothetical trade of Cal Ripken Jr., perhaps the most loyal player of all time and whose name is completely synonymous with the Baltimore Orioles, wouldn't compare because the Orioles don't have an adversary as hated as the Vikings are in Green Bay. This is totally different. Minnesota and Wisconsin just don't get along when it comes to sports. Never have, never will.

> *What Brett Favre did, by coming to Minnesota, is so wrong on so many different levels.*

The thing is, none of the aforementioned, other than Clemens, left to play for a bitter rival. They all went far, far away, to be put out to pasture and retire in peace. Nobody cared when Broadway Joe left the Big Apple, his time was up and he was over the hill. It was more sad than anything else, for a once-shining star to slowly fade and then not be able to let go. And it is different when guys like George Foreman or Lance Armstrong keep coming back, because they compete in individual sports. What makes this so different is the fact that Brett Favre not only went to his former team's archenemy, he *chose* to go there. Remember, he *wanted* to come to Minnesota in 2008 but got dealt to New York instead. It would be different if he were traded to the Vikings, but that wasn't the case. Big difference. That makes it kind of personal in my book. Further, even though he is 40 years old, Favre is not over the hill. Not even close. In fact, he is still widely regarded as a top-10 quarterback in the league. Factor in the guy's durability quotient, and he could keep going for a while. No, he is certainly not the Favre of old, but he is still pretty damn good. Good

Brett Favre answers a question during a news conference prior to his last game as a Packer, a loss to the New York Giants in the NFC Championship Game on January 20, 2008.

enough to be the best quarterback on the Vikings roster for the next two years, anyway.

You see, Brett Favre is the last of the dinosaurs in professional sports. He was the last big-time player to play (almost) his entire career in one city. In an era of über-free agency filled with blood-sucking agents, general managers, and other financial-planning parasites, players today have a whole bunch of mouths to feed and, as such, they come and go like a festering rash. It's in everybody's "best interests" to test the waters elsewhere, or so they would have them believe. The bottom line is that there is very little loyalty in sports. Superstars leave town all the time. Easy come, easy go. That is pro sports today. In just the past few years we have had Kevin Garnett (Timberwolves), Torii Hunter (Twins), and Johan Santana (Twins) all say good-bye to Minnesota. That hurt. Yet we have welcomed Adrian Peterson (Vikings), Joe Mauer (Twins), and Justin Morneau (Twins) in their places. So it ebbs and it flows.

Sure, Favre made a boatload of money with Green Bay, and when he *chose* to re-sign there on several occasions it proved that he wanted to be there. As fans, that makes us feel good. I remember when Twins center fielder Kirby Puckett re-upped with the Twinkies back in '92, right after he led us to our second World Series in five years. I was so jacked. He *wanted* to stay here and he even took less money to do so. How cool was that? We love it when our sacred cows either stay put or come home to pasture. When Paul Molitor came back to Minnesota, I don't think too many Milwaukee Brewers fans got too bent out of shape. Paul is a homegrown St. Paul kid and he wanted to finish his career with the team he grew up rooting for. Same for Dave Winfield and Jack Morris, who also came home for personal reasons to play for the Twins, even giving us the "hometown discount" by playing for less than their market value. Well, Favre's personal reasons aren't the same kind of "personal" in my opinion. They're different. They're more about payback, which is a slippery slope, because in the end the fans are the ones who wind up taking a beating.

In my eyes, Favre has to have a vendetta of some sort. He wants revenge, or at least I think he does. Ted Thompson? Mike McCarthy? It has to be somebody, right? Why the hell else would he be doing all this? Yeah, I know, "the Vikings have a great team and are poised to go to the Super Bowl…" "He is the missing piece…" "He will be playing in a domed stadium…" "He knows the offense so well he could teach it…" "He and Vikings offensive coordinator Darrell Bevell are pals…" "All he has to do is stand back there and hand it off to Adrian Peterson…" I get all of that, but I still ain't buying it. There's got to be more to this than meets the eye.

Introduction: Why I Love to Hate Brett Favre

If Favre wanted to play for the Saints, I am sure Packers fans would have had no problem with that. He grew up just outside of New Orleans rooting for quarterback Archie Manning, who was from Favre's native Mississippi. I am sure they wouldn't have even had a big problem with him going to Dallas, because Favre said a long time ago that his boyhood idol was Cowboys quarterback Roger Staubach. We can give our heroes a free pass for stuff like that because they deserve to be able to play in front of their hometown fans. They want their grannies and granddaddies to come watch them play. I get that. But this is different. Brett Favre has no ties whatsoever to Minnesota. None. Not unless he secretly enjoys subarctic weather and corn dogs on a stick.

> *There are folks in the Dairy State running Favre jerseys through wood chippers.*

I know he says he doesn't care about his legacy, but I have talked to a lot of fans who not only are pissed off beyond recognition, they are deeply and genuinely saddened. For them this was personal. There are folks in the Dairy State running Favre jerseys through wood chippers. Packers fans laughed with him when he hoisted the Lombardi Trophy and they cried with him when his dad died. They were invested. I am not sure what they think the return on that investment should be, but I would imagine it would include his *not* playing for the *one* team that they genuinely hate with the sole intention of getting revenge against his former team.

Packers fans, I would be tempted to tell you that your loss is Minnesota's gain, but I am not ready to go down that road quite yet. In fact, from the way I see it, this could be a win-win for you guys after all. Let's say Favre leads the Vikings to a Super Bowl and they lose. Packers fans are happy because they know Minnesotans will be beside themselves in grief, having lost yet another big game. Let's say Favre leads the Vikings to a Super Bowl and they win. Packers fans can shout across the border that the only reason the Vikings finally won was because they had to borrow *their* quarterback. Either way, I think you're covered.

Plus, how psyched will you be when Minnesota fans find themselves in the same boat you were repeatedly in come the off-season? "Brett, are you going to come back? Are you going to retire?" Sound familiar? I'm sure it's coming. And no, Minnesota doesn't have an heir apparent waiting in the wings like you did in Aaron Rodgers. *So this is all about this team winning right now.* The way I see it, if Favre can lead Minnesota to a Super Bowl, then the Vikings will probably get a new stadium. If not, there's a strong possibility that the team will be renamed the Los Angeles Vikings. And I know that as much as Packer Nation hates this team, even they don't want to see that happen. At least I hope not...

I'll be honest. As a Vikings fan, I love the drama. In a sick, sadistic kind of way it makes me happy when Packers fans are miserable. Misery loves company, and believe me, I've had plenty of purple hangovers through the years. You see, I went to school at the University of Minnesota and became friends with a ton of die-hard Packers fans, many of whom were fraternity brothers and wound up staying in the area after college. As such, the ribbing back and forth with my cheesehead brethren is endless. I think the whole situation is wonderful because Vikings fans haven't had a whole lot to cheer about in recent memory. In fact, we had to live vicariously through Green Bay's Super Bowl back in '97. And trust me, *we heard about that* over and over again.

> *How psyched will you be when Minnesota fans find themselves in the same boat you were repeatedly in come the off-season? "Brett, are you going to come back? Are you going to retire?" Sound familiar?*

Look, you have pain, we have pain. Does the name Herschel Walker ring a bell? Or how about Denny Green taking a knee in '98 in the NFC Championship Game? Or who could forget the infamous "Hail Mary?" I was only six years old when Dallas beat my Vikes to win the divisional playoffs back in 1975, but I can still remember it as if it were yesterday. I remember watching the game in our basement and seeing my dad and two brothers going ballistic when Drew Pearson miraculously caught the game-winning touchdown from Roger Staubach after clearly pushing off cornerback Nate Wright. And yes, he *did* push off. The fans went nuts. One drunk lunatic even heaved a whiskey bottle off of the third deck of old Metropolitan Stadium and hit the referee in the head just moments after the big play. Luckily, it didn't kill the guy, but if it had, I think a lot of folks up here would have considered it to be "justifiable homicide." I even remember hearing afterward about how Fran Tarkenton's dad, whose name was ironically "Dallas," tragically dropped dead of a heart attack while watching the game on TV immediately after the play. You just can't make this stuff up. Maybe we're cursed?

Yes, you have pain, but there is a big difference. Green Bay has won, like, a bazillion championships—12, to be exact, most in NFL history. We have exactly zero. We're desperate. So desperate in fact that we will even start rooting for Brett Favre. Call me crazy, but I have officially gone from hating Brett Favre to loving him. I even took Favre on my fantasy-football team this year for the first time in more than 15 seasons of play. I caught hell for it from my buddies, too: "You homer!" "What a dick!" It doesn't feel right, but a guy's gotta do what a guy's gotta do.

Truth be told, I have actually rooted for the Packers at least twice. The first time, they were playing Dallas, years ago, and we needed the Cowboys to lose in order for us to make the playoffs. It was *really weird*. Kind of creepy, in fact. The other time was actually back in 1998, when the Pack wound up losing to Denver in Super Bowl XXXII. This was sort of a lose-lose proposition for me as a Vikings fan. If the Pack won, then I would have to hear about it from all my Wisconsin buddies, which I had already sort of been used to at that point because Green Bay had just won the big game the year before. On the other hand, however, if Denver lost, then that would have given them the record. Record? You see, I want somebody else to hold the dubious distinction of "Most Super Bowl Losses." We have four, Buffalo has four, and at the time Denver had four. Sadly, John Elway put an end to that as he led the Broncos to a pair of titles in '98 and '99. As such, that leaves just us and Buffalo. So go Bills!…until you make it to the Super Bowl, that is.

In many regards, writing this book was really therapeutic—for me and for the legions of players, media personalities, and fans I spoke to. In the process, I learned a lot about Brett Favre. They guy has certainly lived a fascinating life. No kidding. Having said that, I want to say that this book is not even close to being a definitive history, nor is it a trashy tell-all. Rather, it is a fun behind-the-scenes look into what I feel is at the core of the greatest rivalry in football. The emotions are raw and real because I started writing the book about a month before he signed with the Vikings. Yeah, I knew he'd skip camp and sign, that's one of the "Brett Rules" that you'll learn about. Brett doesn't *do* training camp, at least not at this stage of his career.

Because of the timing, this book turned out to be a snapshot that captured the pure essence of just what everybody thought about Favre's monumental decision. The vile reactions and honest opinions are wonderful. In all, I interviewed more than 100 current and former players, current and former Favre teammates, coaches, referees, media personalities, and fans. I even spoke to Brett on a couple of occasions, albeit briefly, in the Vikings locker room. We made small talk, and I gave him a few of my books to read. I was hoping to interview him in-depth but was shot down pretty quickly by his handlers. I felt better after one of the Vikings media relations guys told me that he just turned down David Letterman and Conan O'Brien, as well, so at least I was in good company. I did get to talk at length with a few of his close friends, though, including Vikings kicker Ryan Longwell, who provided a lot of great insight.

As I learned more and more about No. 4, I began to understand him better, not only as a player but as a person. He has been through a lot over the years. After months of extensive research about this guy, I came to the conclusion that it all starts and stops with his toughness.

That is what this guy is all about when you get to the very core of it. Mental toughness and physical toughness. He is as tough as they come and he has the numbers to prove it. So I thought it would be appropriate to go back and take a closer look at how he grew up and find out just where all of that toughness came from.

Green Bay has won, like, a bazillion championships.... We have exactly zero. We're desperate. So desperate in fact that we will even start rooting for Brett Favre.

The Pride of Kiln...

Brett Lorenzo Favre was born on October 10, 1969, in Gulfport, Mississippi, the second of four children, and raised near the small one-stoplight town of Kiln. He grew up on more than 50 acres of land between Mill Creek and Rotten Bayou. All that land meant plenty of space for the Favre boys—Scott, Brett, and Jeff—along with sister Brandi, to play ball and beat the hell out of each other. Whether it was hunting or fishing or playing baseball or football, they were out there 24/7, wrestling, throwing, competing, and having fun. Brett's dad, Irv, was an outstanding athlete who had been a pitcher on the Southern Mississippi University baseball team. He was a hard-nosed high school football coach and about as tough a customer as they come. He didn't raise any wimps, that was for sure. Tom Kertscher's book *Favre: A Packer Fan's Tribute* describes Irv's tough love remedy. If one of the kids got hurt, regardless of the injury, his answer was usually the same: "Put some ice on it." That was always Big Irv's solution for everything. "If you get hurt, you crawl off the field," he once told Brett. "When you can't crawl off the field, I'll come get you."

Brett's mom, Bonita, a special education teacher, would cook mountains of food for her active kids, after they'd played for hours in the hot sun. For as long as Brett could remember, sports were always an integral part of the Favre household. "I was three when I got my first football uniform, including the helmet and shoulder pads, for

Christmas," wrote Favre in his 2004 biography. "I got a baseball uniform shortly afterward. We were always throwing a ball of some sort around. We loved playing football in the yard. It was brutal. We used to take a hose, water down the yard, and put our football pads on. Then we'd get after it. We'd be flying around in the mud, knocking the heck out of each other. We played tackle football with whoever was around. Usually it was just the three boys. Noses got smashed. Fingers got mangled. There was blood. But there were never too many fights. There was a lot of arguing and shoving. We'd get ticked at each other, but that was it. We'd argue and the next day we'd be right out there again like nothing ever happened. One game we made up as kids to pass the time was called Goal Line. Scott and I would play defense, and Jeff would play offense. We gave Jeff the ball five yards from the goal line, and he had to try to score in four plays. And there was no running around us. Jeff had to run through us to score. We used to beat the heck out of him. God, we played that game all the time, even when Scott was in college.

> *On the night before the game, Favre and his roommate...sat up in their dorm together pounding beers. Neither had seen any playing time and figured they weren't about to any time soon, so they proceeded to get sloshed.*

Here's Jeff, about 13, and his two big brothers pounding on him. We busted each other up pretty good. But that's what we did for fun."

As a fire-balling pitcher, Favre started on the baseball team as an eighth-grader and earned five varsity letters playing baseball and football at Hancock North Central High School. On the gridiron, he lined up all over the place, at quarterback, safety, kicker, and punter. His dad had long ago installed the wishbone offense after attending a coaching clinic conducted by legendary Alabama coach Bear Bryant, who said it was the only way to go. Favre was a good high school quarterback, but was never able to shine in the shadow of his father's ultraconservative, run-oriented offense, rarely throwing more than five passes in a game. Brett's older brother, Scott, had already gone on to play quarterback for Mississippi State, so he was optimistic that he too would be able to play the game at the next level. Big Irv thought his boy had what it took to play college ball, so he put in a phone call to his alma mater to see if one of the scouts would give him a look. They agreed.

Looking at his stat sheet, which included very few passing yards, things did not look very promising for young Brett. It was clear that he was a good athlete, however, so Southern Miss offered him a scholarship—the only one he would receive. With that, Favre graduated from high school in 1987 and headed 50 miles north to Hattiesburg to start his freshman year. Once at Southern Miss, Favre insisted upon playing quarterback, despite the fact that he would start the season as a seventh-stringer on the team's depth chart. He wasted little time in making a name for himself, though, and quickly caught the attention of the coaches during practice when he would routinely throw 80-yard bombs down the field with pin-point accuracy. His big break would eventually come in a pretty dubious manner.

On the night before the game, Favre and his roommate, Chris Ryals, sat up in their dorm together pounding beers. Neither had seen any playing time and figured they weren't about to any time soon, so they proceeded to get sloshed.

"We sat there and just got drunk, drunk, drunk," Ryals said in a 2005 interview with the *Milwaukee Journal Sentinel.* "We figured if we drank eight beers, then seven, then six…we figured 36 would make the perfect pyramid. We drank a case and a half. That was in the good old days of Johnny Carson and David Lettermen. We sat there like two old men, watching TV and drinking beer. Oh, it was beautiful. We completed the pyramid about 2:15 in the morning."

The next day, the Golden Eagles hosted Tulane at M.M. Roberts Stadium. According to Ryals, Favre was paying the price for pyramiding on the eve of a big game. "When we ran on the field, he went over to the wall and bent over and ralphed," said Ryals. "Just vomits his guts up right there. He looks like he's about to drop warming up. He's sweating bullets, white as a sheet."

Frustrated by his offense's lack of productivity, in the third quarter of the game coach Jim Carmody rolled the dice and instructed his offensive coordinator to put in the 17-year-old freshman at quarterback. A startled Favre jumped at the opportunity and ran onto the field.

"All five offensive linemen were fifth-year seniors, and now you've got this young idiot quarterback," Ryals continued. "He was hungover. Sick. They all knew he got drunk the night before."

Favre made the most of his opportunity that afternoon, however, throwing two touchdown passes en route to leading the team to a dramatic 31–24 come-from-behind victory. Coach Carmody had found himself a quarterback, and thus began the Brett Favre era at Southern Miss, a memorable four-year run that produced a 29–17 record, a pair of bowl bids, and upset victories over nationally ranked Alabama, Auburn, and Florida State. Midway through Favre's sophomore season Favre became a father when his longtime high-school girlfriend, Deanna, gave birth to their daughter, Brittany. "I was 18 and Deanna was 19 when she got pregnant," Favre later said to *Playboy* magazine. "People say, 'You damn ass, making her look bad. Why didn't you marry her?' But we weren't ready for that. We never would have made it. Five years later we'd be like 90 percent of the people who get married for that reason—divorced and hating each other."

Favre's senior year almost never happened. On July 14, 1990, he was involved in a near-fatal car accident. While driving around a curvy bend near his parents' house, Favre lost control of his car and flipped it three times, end over end, before it finally came to rest against a tree. With the car badly mangled, his brother was able to smash a window with a golf club in order for Brett to be evacuated to the hospital. Once there, doctors removed more than two feet of his small intestine. Incredibly, just six weeks later, on September 8, Favre, now 40 pounds lighter, led Southern Miss to a comeback victory over Alabama.

"You can call it a miracle or a legend or whatever you want to," said Alabama coach Gene Stallings in a 2002 *Sports Illustrated* interview. "I just know that on that day, Brett Favre was larger than life."

Favre, who graduated with a teaching degree in special education in 1991, ultimately set several school passing records, including career touchdown passes (52), completions (613), attempts (1,169), and total offense (7,606 yards). From there he was drafted by the Atlanta Falcons in the second round (33rd overall) of the '91 NFL Draft. That July he agreed to a three-year, $1.4 million contract with a reported signing bonus of $350,000. Favre's first pass in an NFL regular-season game resulted in an interception returned for a touchdown. He only attempted four others that season, completing none of them. The 21-year-old Favre was doing too much partying and not nearly enough studying. Needless to say, the combination of Favre moving to the big city and getting paid a boatload of cash would not prove to be a good combination.

> *"[Atlanta] coach Jerry Glanville... once said during an exhibition game that it would take a plane crash for him to put Favre into the game."*
> *—Tom Silverstein*

"In Atlanta, Favre had become a whipping boy for flamboyant coach Jerry Glanville, who never approved of [general manager Ken] Herock's decision to draft him and once said during an exhibition game that it would take a plane crash for him to put Favre into the game," wrote Tom Silverstein of the *Milwaukee Journal Sentinel*. "The more Glanville ignored the wild and unbridled Favre, the more Favre rebelled. Favre's behavior was immature and unprofessional. He stayed out late, he showed up late, and fell asleep in meetings. Glanville thought so little of Favre that he refused to make him Pro Bowl quarterback Chris Miller's backup, and Herock was forced to trade for Billy Joe Tolliver."

Seeing nothing but potential, that off-season Green Bay Packers general manager Ron Wolf took a huge leap of faith and traded the team's first-round pick (19th overall) for Favre. Wolf had intended to take Favre in the 1991 draft, but came up one pick short to the Falcons. He wasn't going to let him get away this time. With that,

Brett Favre heaves an awkward, desperate pass toward one of his teammates in a playoff loss to the St. Louis Rams in 2002. *Photo courtesy of Getty Images*

Favre headed north to Green Bay, where he joined Mike Tomczak and Ty Detmer in competing for the backup role to starting quarterback Don Majkowski. As fate would have it, midway through the third game of the '92 season against Cincinnati at Lambeau Field, Majkowski tore a ligament in his ankle that would put him on the shelf for four weeks. Favre was given the green light to step in, and he wanted to make an immediate impact. Nervous, he choked. In fact, after fumbling four times during the course of the game, the crowd starting chanting for Detmer to be put in. Favre hung tough, though, and dug in. Down 23–17 with just over a minute to go in the game, he led an improbable comeback that included a 42-yard strike to Sterling Sharpe followed by what proved to be the game-winning touchdown pass to Kitrick Taylor with 13 seconds left on the clock.

The next week Favre got the start as he led the Pack to a 17–3 victory over the Pittsburgh Steelers. With it began the longest consecutive-starts streak for a quarterback in NFL history. Favre would remain as the starter for the rest of the season, leading the team to a 9–7 record and narrowly missing the play-offs on their last game. He would finish the season with 3,227 yards and a quarterback rating of 85.3, good enough to earn him a trip to his first Pro Bowl. The next year Favre led Green Bay to its to first playoff appearance since '82 and was named to his second Pro Bowl.

Favre...wanted to make an immediate impact. Nervous, he choked. In fact, after fumbling four times...the crowd starting chanting for [Ty] Detmer to be put in.

For his efforts, Favre was awarded a five-year, $19 million contract. The kid from Mississippi had officially arrived.

In all, Favre spent 16 seasons in Green Bay, never missing a start along the way, despite a slew of personal problems that at times came in waves. His first big test came in 1996, when he went to treatment for his addiction to the painkiller Vicodin. Favre's drug problems first came about following a separated left shoulder he suffered while being sacked by Reggie White during a game against the Philadelphia Eagles back in November 1992. "Vikes," as they are called, are well known for their potential for addiction.

"Some players take it and get sick to their stomach, so they don't do it again," Favre wrote in his 1997 autobiography *Favre: For the Record*. "Other players think it feels pretty good but they'd never take it enough to get addicted. Then there are players like me, who take it and get hooked."

> *Favre's behavior was immature and unprofessional. He stayed out late, he showed up late, and fell asleep in meetings.*

By the '95 season Favre was popping as many as 15 pills a day, getting the narcotics mostly from teammates who had no problem enabling their star player. Now fully dependent, Favre would sometimes throw up the pills, only to pick them back up and force them down again and again.

"He was plagued by many of the drug's side effects," wrote Gary D'Amato of the *Milwaukee Journal Sentinel*. "He was constantly dehydrated, acutely constipated—he often went a week or longer between bowel movements—and endured bouts of nausea and vomiting. He choked down the pills at precisely 9:00 each night, and when they kicked in, he was so wired up he paced the house or played video games until the early morning hours, while an increasingly suspicious Deanna slept fitfully upstairs."

He eventually tried to kick it but simply couldn't. In February 1996 Favre suffered a seizure following a minor procedure to have bone spurs removed from his ankle. Worried that the seizure was a side effect from the Vicodin, Favre, also a heavy drinker, finally agreed to meet with some NFL-appointed doctors. They urged him to seek professional help, but Favre refused. Eventually, after several failed attempts to get him to commit himself, the league classified Favre as "behavioral-referred" instead of "self-referred," which meant that according to league rules, he had to either get help or pay fines equivalent to four weeks of pay, nearly $900,000 in salary. The Packers organization was stunned to hear the news of his addiction.

With that, Favre reported to the Menninger Clinic in Topeka, Kansas. He stayed for 46 days and, while there, he proposed to Deanna. They married that July, just prior to training camp. Clean and sober, Favre thought his troubles were behind him. Just a short while later, however, it was learned that Favre's sister, Brandi, had been involved in aiding a drive-by shooting. Not too long after that his older brother, Scott, was convicted of felony drunken driving after hitting a railroad crossing. The accident ultimately took the life of Scott Favre's passenger, Mark Harvy, one of Brett's best friends.

Things eventually improved, and Favre stayed strong. So strong, in fact, that the next season he led the Packers all the way to a Super Bowl victory over the New England Patriots. Making it even sweeter was the fact that it was in Favre's backyard of New Orleans. Favre would also win the league MVP award that season, his third straight, after throwing for 3,899 yards and an NFC record 39 touchdown passes. After the big game, Favre looked back on the year during an interview with *Sports Illustrated*. "Through everything I really believed I'd be here today, talking about being world champions," he said. "My best friend's gone forever. Trouble never seems to be far away, and the future won't be all rosy, but they can't take this away from me. Thirty years from now, the kids will be getting ready for Super Bowl 61, and NFL Films will drag out Steve Sabol—he'll be around 102 then—and he'll talk about how Brett Favre fought through such adversity. And there will be other players and coaches. But I know this: we etched our place in history today."

Favre would go through his share of ups and downs over the ensuing years. The team did well, and it was a relatively uneventful time as far as tragedies went in his personal life. That all changed on December 21, 2003, however, when Favre's dad, Irv, passed away of a massive heart attack. He was 58. Despite having a fractured right thumb, Favre decided to play in a game that next night against Oakland, figuring his dad would want it no other way. "It's almost like

I could hear my dad: 'Boy, don't worry about me. I'm fine,'" Favre told *Sports Illustrated*'s Peter King.

In his book, Tom Kertscher relates how, before the game, an emotional Favre addressed his teammates: "I loved my dad, I love football, I love you guys," he said. "I grew up playing baseball for my dad, and I grew up playing football for my dad. It's all I know. It's my life. I'm playing in this game because I've invested too much in the game, in you, in this team, not to play. If you ever doubted my commitment to this team, never doubt it again."

And so, with the hearts of millions behind him, Favre went out and tossed four touchdowns on nearly 400 yards passing en route to beating the Raiders 41–7. It was a game, wrote Bob McGinn of the *Milwaukee Journal Sentinel*, that passed immediately into legend.

More tragedy would come for Favre in 2004, when his wife Deanna's 24-year-old younger brother, Casey Tynes, died in an all-terrain vehicle accident on Favre's property near Hattiesburg. Then, less than a week later, Deanna was diagnosed with breast cancer.

"I've found myself over the last 24 hours a couple times saying, 'Why me?' or, 'Why of all places … ,'" said Favre in a 2005 Associated Press article. "As quickly as that thought pops in my head—and it probably pops in my head more than I'd like it to—I try to remind myself of the things to be thankful for, which there are a lot."

Deanna would recover, but the same could not be said for Favre's family home in Kiln after Hurricane Katrina stuck the Gulf Coast in 2005. Favre's mother and grandmother reportedly spent the evening in the family attic after the house filled up with water within a matter of minutes. Sadly, the home was destroyed. Favre's home on nearly 500 acres of land in Hattiesburg, an hour north of Kiln, suffered extensive damage, as well.

With far too many broken bones, sprains, torn muscles, bruises, and contusions to speak of, to say that Favre is tough would be quite an understatement. *Men's Journal* even named him the "Toughest Guy in America" in 2004. In the article it listed some of his past injuries, including a first-degree separation of his left shoulder in

1992, a deep thigh bruise in 1993, a severely bruised left hip in 1994, right elbow tendinitis in 2000, a left foot sprain in 2000, a sprained lateral collateral ligament in his left knee in 2002, a broken right thumb in 2003, and a torn biceps tendon and rotator cuff in 2008, just to name a few. Favre wrote about his legendary toughness in his 2004 autobiography:

> Fans ask how I've been able to play for so long without missing a game. The easy answer is to say that it's because I'm so doggone tough, or as Mike Holmgren would say, because I'm so doggone hard-headed. The truth is it's probably a combination of things. I've been fortunate to play on winning teams with good offensive lines. I also tend to recoil, or step back, almost immediately after I throw a pass. I'm pretty sure that has kept my legs from getting tangled up under more than one pile. The Streak isn't all about durability, though. It's about ability, too. Nobody plays in 208 straight games just because they didn't get hurt. A player has to be good enough, for a long enough time, to keep earning the starting job. Nothing's ever handed to anyone in this league, but sometimes all a player needs is a chance. I got mine when Don Majkowski sprained his ankle, and if I hadn't, who knows how things would have turned out? That's one reason I try my best to play no matter how bad the injury. I don't want to give anyone the chance that Majik gave me. I also feel like I owe it to my coaches, teammates, and fans

> *"Thirty years from now, the kids will be getting ready for Super Bowl 61, and NFL Films will drag out Steve Sabol—he'll be around 102 then—and he'll talk about how Brett Favre fought through such adversity."*
> —*Brett Favre*

to show up on Sunday. I don't want to let them down because I know how much it means to them, and I feel like they know how much it means to me, too.

As for the streak, Favre set the NFL record for quarterbacks back in November 1999 at Lambeau Field when he started his 117th con- secutive game. Incredibly, 10 years and 153 starts later, Favre broke former Vikings defensive end Jim Marshall's record of 270 consecutive regular-season starts on September 20, 2009, in a game against the Lions at Detroit—truly making him the NFL's all-time iron man. Some would argue that Giants punter Jeff Feagles can make that claim with 338 consecutive starts (as of September 2009), but the reality is that punters simply don't count.

> ESPN's Gene Wojciechowski even accused Favre of committing "cheesehead treason," and compared him to Fredo Corleone in The Godfather: Part II.

"I think the fact that anyone can do it is amazing," said a humbled Favre to the *Star Tribune* of Marshall's streak. "I think just playing in the NFL, period, is an honor and something that is very hard to do. But what Jim did—and you can talk about the game was smaller then, it wasn't as fast, or the seasons were shorter—it's still football, and you still have to play in every one of those games, and in his case be physical and hit or be hit. To even be mentioned with some of the greatest players to ever play this game regardless of position—no matter how long I've played or honors I've received—I'm honored more than anything to be mentioned in the same breath with guys like that."

Looking Forward...

So this leads us back to Favre eventually coming to Minnesota. If you want to learn about the genesis of why Favre left Green Bay, flip the book over, it's all there—conspiracy theories and all. Meanwhile, let's continue discussing why I, like so many others, love to hate Brett Favre. While it's tough not to love the guy for his actions on the field, it's his actions off the field that elicit such vile and passionate reactions. From the incessant retiring and unretiring, to the fact that he *chose* to play for the rival Vikings—seemingly everybody has an opinion about No. 4.

ESPN's Gene Wojciechowski even accused Favre of committing "cheesehead treason," and compared him to Fredo Corleone in *The Godfather: Part II*—the son who betrays the family. He then compares Packers fans, meanwhile, to Michael Corleone, who tells his older brother, "Fredo, you're nothing to me now."

And speaking of the Godfather, here's a crazy one. According to the *Winona* (Minnesota) *Daily News*, shortly after Favre signed with Minnesota, a woman came into a Tires Plus store needing a new belt for her Chevy Malibu. Hearing crying and bahhing coming from the trunk, the service guys started to get concerned, so they called her on it. Fearing the worst, they were dumbfounded when she opened the trunk and out popped a purple goat that had been bound and spray painted, complete with a No. 4 shaved into his side. She then informed the men that she was about to take the animal off to be "slaughtered." The repair shop immediately called animal control, who intercepted the woman as she left the shop, and they took the goat into protective custody. You can't help but be reminded of the infamous scene in *The Godfather* with the horse's head. I mean, what was this woman going to do? I can only imagine Brett rolling over in his big bed and suddenly, *BAAAHH*!

> She opened the trunk and out popped a purple goat that had been bound and spray painted, complete with a No. 4 shaved into his side.

Even Hall of Fame Vikings quarterback Fran Tarkenton jumped on the anti-Favre bandwagon in an interview with the *Star Tribune*. "I think it's despicable. What he put the Packers through last year was not good," he said.

"Here's an organization that was loyal to him, provided stability, provided players. It just wasn't about Brett Favre. In this day and time, we have glorified the Brett Favres of the world so much, they think it's about them. He goes to New York and bombs. He's 39 years old. How would you like Ray Nitschke in his last year [playing for] the Vikings, or I retire and go play for the

> "I think it's despicable. What he put the Packers through last year was not good."
> —Fran Tarkenton

Packers? ... Playing quarterback is about the relationships you have with your coaches, with your players, with your trainers, with your managers. How can you do that if you show up on game day and you haven't put the time in? ... He's been a great player, there's no question about it, but it's all about him. It is supposed to be all about your team."

The whole "Favreapalooza" experience has been pretty surreal. One of the things that has truly amazed me in this entire debacle is just how quickly people on this side of the border have embraced him. This guy was the sworn enemy for a lot of years over here, and now we are loving him up like nobody's business. And it's not just Vikings fans, tons of transplanted cheeseheads who now live over here have embraced him, too. Maybe they put something in the water so that we would all fall in love with him?

I know several hard-core Vikings fans who have been deprogrammed, including one of my good buddies, Mike Rendahl. Mikey is a lifelong Vikings season-ticket holder of more than 40 years who, like myself, used to loathe Brett Favre. Trust me, I sat there alongside him at the Dome for many a game over the years, right there with his kid brother Todd, cursing the hated Pack. As I was writing the book, I asked him to please give me a quote or two about his feelings regarding Favre signing with the purple. Fully expecting a profanity-laced tirade, to my astonishment what I got was an eloquent, articulate, thoughtful soliloquy. Obviously, somebody or something has gotten to him. Read it for yourself:

Introduction: Why I Love to Hate Brett Favre

Sure, I can tell you as a Vikings fan that I hated Brett Favre for years, but in reality it's just drama because deep down I have always admired the man for his passion, competitiveness, and dedication to the game. In a perfect world, Favre playing for the Vikings isn't good for the game, but the game has changed, and that's not his fault. In a very selfish way, I cannot believe that after all these years I am looking at this legend in a Vikings uniform and I have to admit it's one hell of an honor as a fan to have him on our team—and it's even better knowing that he wants to be here. In the end, Favre will forever go down as a Packer, and that's just the way it has to be. But for now he's a Viking, and I'm going to enjoy it while it lasts!

You see? The poor bastard has been drinking the purple Kool-Aid for so long that he has simply gone nuts. Sorry dude, you know we'll always be pals, but your newly found forbidden "bro-mance" for No. 4 just made me throw up in my mouth. Has Brett Favre secretly brainwashed us somehow, like that poor sap from the *Manchurian Candidate*? I hate the fact that I just had to throw poor Mikey under the bus like that, but I put the blame squarely on the shoulders of Mr. Favre.

Here are some other things I hate about Brett Favre:

I hate the fact that even though I didn't want to, I actually liked Favre's cameo in the classic Farrelly brothers movie *There's Something About Mary*. That scene where he enters a room and Healy (played by Matt Dillon) says, "What the hell is Brett Favre doing here?" to which he replies, "I'm in town to play the Dolphins, you dumb-ass!" is a classic. Ted (played by Ben Stiller), who sadly had to skip prom after getting his "man business" caught in his zipper, has the best one-liner in the movie when he mispronounces Favre's name and says, "What about Brett Faahv-ruh?" To this day, that is still how most die-hard Vikings fans refer to him.

I hate the fact that Favre broke Dan Marino's all-time touchdown passing record on our turf at the Dome. It happened on September 30,

2007, when he threw No. 421, a 16-yarder to Greg Jennings to set the record.

I hate all the Brett Favre jokes that have gone viral on the Internet since he signed with Minnesota. If I get one more of those stupid "Cash for Clunkers" cartoons, I may have to hurl. Not all of them are as annoying, though. I enjoyed the one about us changing our name from Vikings to "Vicodins"—hey, now that he's clean and sober, I think it's safe to go there. In fact, I think that's so funny that I hate the fact that I didn't come up with it myself.

I hate all the Brett Favre clichés that people are using to describe him now: "grizzled veteran," "field general," "gunslinger," and my personal favorite: "He's just a big kid who just loves to play the game." Hey, I am just as guilty of using this crap throughout the pages of this book, but I still hate it. Although I have to admit, I liked the description of him as a "one-time icon turned self-absorbed football nomad." Good stuff.

I hate the fact that Brett Favre can wear Wranglers, drive a tractor, and do Sears commercials—and hot chicks still think he's all that.

I hate the speculation that Favre had either somehow helped out the Detroit Lions or actually wanted to play for them. It's ludicrous. Back in the summer of 2008 it was reported that Favre had spoken at length with then–Lions president Matt Millen. While some pontificated that Favre was passing along inside information to help the Lions beat the Packers that season, like some sort of CIA scare, others thought he was trying to lobby Millen to trade for him—so he could stick it to the Pack. In reality, they texted about rodents. That's right. "We texted back and forth," Millen said in an MLIVE.com interview. "I told him I had a groundhog getting into my vegetable garden so I shot him. He said 'Mmm, make a stew.'"

I hate all of the incessant speculation we had to endure about whether he would eventually join the Vikings or not. I am thrilled that it is finally over. From the ESPN tweet leaks to the rumors to the innuendos—it was all just so over the top.

I hate all the talk about his retiring and unretiring. I don't have a big problem with all of that. For me, it was more about the fact that he turned on his loyal fans. I thought one blogger had an interesting take: "Once upon a time, we hated quitters. Now, apparently, we hate guys who won't quit. In a country where we've extended our workplace hours and mandatory age of retirement, why are we suddenly in a dither when a guy on the cusp of turning 40 wants to keep working?" Right on, brother.

I hate the fact that the media doesn't talk too much about all the charity work he has done. Over the last 10 years his Fourward Foundation has donated in excess of $3 million to disadvantaged and disabled children in Wisconsin and Mississippi. For that the guy should be commended.

> *The poor bastard has been drinking the purple Kool-Aid for so long that he has simply gone nuts...your newly found forbidden "bro-mance" for No. 4 just made me throw up in my mouth.*

"If you really think about it, that stuff is so much more important than football," said Favre in a 2008 onmilwaukee.com interview. "But at times we lose sight of that. For me, football has been wonderful in a lot of ways, but the fact that I've been able to touch other people's lives, and Deanna has said this I don't know how many times, that you don't realize the impact you have on people, I really don't. I've never really thought about it. All I've thought about was playing football and playing it a certain way, and whatever comes along with that, great. Whether it be money, commercials, reaching out to people, charity, whatever. It's because of football, I'm well aware of that. But because of football, I've been impacted by a lot of people and charities. I am very proud of the things that we have done off the field. Could we have done more? Sure. Could we all do more? Absolutely. But we have impacted other people's lives in a positive way, I would hope, and we are thankful for that."

I love the fact that Packers general manager Ted Thompson was voted by his peers as the NFL Executive of the Year in 2008. Seriously, congratulations. Thompson, a 10-year player with the Houston Oilers, has been made out to be the villain in this whole fiasco, so I hope he feels vindicated. I am sure a lot of Packers fans who are still up in arms about Favre leaving, however, will hate that he won the award.

I hate the fact that I was not able to interview Bart Starr for this book. I tried and tried, but he just didn't want to comment on it. He said it was just too personal for him and he apologized for that, but he refused to talk on the record about Favre. I respect that.

> Favre was "sacked" by the defensive end [Michael Strahan]...and looked pathetic on the play, laying down and rolling over like a sick puppy.

I hate how a lot of the older players who I interviewed for the book talked about being loyal to their teams, yet in reality, because they didn't have free agency in those days, I am sure most of them would have played for the enemy in a heartbeat if offered a boatload of cash. Sad, hypocritical, yet true.

I hate the fact that Brett Favre totally sandbagged it and took a dive for his buddy, Michael Strahan. It came in the regular-season finale of 2001, when, in a game against the New York Giants at Giants Stadium, Favre was "sacked" by the defensive end. It was Strahan's lone sack of the game and gave him the NFL's single-season sack record of 22.5, which topped Jets defensive end Mark Gastineau's record of 22 set in 1984. Favre looked pathetic on the play, laying down and rolling over like a sick puppy. Fans were split; some thought it was a classy thing to do for his friend, while others contended it was a "disgraceful dive that tarnished the integrity of both men."

"I know a lot has been made of it, but like I said, I have done that numerous times this year," Favre said to SI.com of changing the play from a handoff without telling his teammates. "People can say what they want, but no second thoughts.... There is bigger fish to fry than something like that. Life goes on. At least for us it does."

I hate the analogy that Favre playing in Minnesota is like that of Elvis Presley in his later years, when he was all fat and drugged up, hanging on to his lounge-lizard act in Vegas with all of his loyal fans still proclaiming him to be the King. Look, if this guy comes up here and stinks up the joint, I am going to be crushed. We need the young, skinny, "ain't nuthin but a hound dog" Elvis, not the over-the-hill, size-56 leisure-suit one. I, like so many other fans, just want him to play well, stay healthy, and understand the concept of "knowing when it's time to take the keys away from grandpa."

Case in point, back in the early '80s Raiders great Kenny Stabler finished his career with the New Orleans Saints. The "Snake," as he was affectionately known by his legions of fans, was old and tired, yet couldn't let go. As a young teenager, Favre went to go see the iconic quarterback play at the nearby Louisiana Superdome. He remembers the day well and commented on how it would one day have an impact on when he would "know" when to finally hang it up. (Oh, yeah, and I hate the following quote, too.)

> We need the young, skinny, "ain't nuthin but a hound dog" Elvis, not the over-the-hill, size-56 leisure-suit one.

"I couldn't wait to see Kenny Stabler come out of the locker room," Favre told the *Wisconsin State Journal* back in 2005. "He came out, and his hair was all long, his uniform was hanging off of him—his better days were behind him. I just remember, to the fans, he was just the savior. Boy, once they got him in New Orleans, he was going to turn them around. Well, that didn't happen. So I'd hate to go somewhere else and have everybody say, 'Hey, we've got Brett.' I mean, too many great things have happened for me here [with the Packers]. And if it ends tomorrow, it ends tomorrow. But I don't need to go somewhere else and prove anything.... I don't see myself like a Kenny Stabler. No offense to him, he had a great career and he was a great quarterback.

Brett Favre's Bottom 10 Career Moments
Source: Don Gulbrandsen, author and managing editor, Triumph Books

1. THE UGLY END
DATE: January 20, 2008
SCORE: Giants 23, Packers 20
WHY IT MATTERED: On a frigid night in Green Bay, with a Super Bowl berth on the line, Favre faded badly in the second half of the NFC Championship Game. He ended his Packers career with an ugly overtime interception to Corey Webster that the Giants converted into the game-winning field goal. Favre said good-bye to Green Bay looking old, cold, and indifferent.

2. QB MATCHUP MELTDOWN
DATE: January 21, 2002
SCORE: Rams 45, Packers 17
WHY IT MATTERED: The hype for the Brett Favre vs. Kurt Warner showdown in the NFC Playoffs was huge, but Favre delivered one of the worst postseason quarterbacking performances in history, tossing six interceptions, two returned for touchdowns.

3. HUMILIATED BY THE VIKES
DATE: January 9, 2005
SCORE: Vikings 31, Packers 17
WHY IT MATTERED: Minnesota visited Lambeau Field as a lightly regarded, 8–8 wild-card team; the Packers were division champs and on a late-season roll. Favre responded with yet another playoff stinker, throwing four interceptions. The bad taste of this game carried over into a disastrous 2005 and led to the firing of coach Mike Sherman.

4. OUTPLAYED BY VICK
DATE: January 4, 2003
SCORE: Falcons 27, Packers 7
WHY IT MATTERED: As NFC North champs, the Packers were a big favorite going into this wild-card match-up. Green Bay never got on track offensively, Atlanta jumped out to a big lead, and Favre killed any second-half comeback attempt with poor play, a lost fumble, and an interception in Green Bay's first home playoff loss in history.

5. A GROUNDED JET
DATE: December 28, 2008
SCORE: Dolphins 24, Jets 17
WHY IT MATTERED: Favre performed poorly in his last five games with the Jets, but the season-ending loss to Miami is the one that stung. Favre was acquired to take the team to the playoffs, still a possibility with a win *continues*

in this game, but he couldn't seal the deal. Instead he tossed three interceptions, including one that went for a Dolphins TD.

6. Un-Grand Reopening

DATE: September 7, 2003
SCORE: Vikings 30, Packers 25
WHY IT MATTERED: The 2003 home opener was supposed to be a huge celebration to dedicate a renovated Lambeau Field, but Favre's four interceptions (including three in the first half) helped Minnesota take a big lead the Packers couldn't overcome.

7. Taking a Dive

DATE: January 6, 2002
SCORE: Packers 34, Giants 25
WHY IT MATTERED: When Favre intentionally ran into the arms of his buddy Michael Strahan—giving the Giants' defensive end the NFL single-season sack record—he created a firestorm of debate. Though it didn't affect the outcome of the game, it sure left a bad taste in people's mouths.

8. Welcome to the Metrodome

DATE: December 27, 1992
SCORE: Vikings 27, Packers 7
WHY IT MATTERED: Favre's first trip to his future home field is one he's

probably blocked from his memory. With a chance to propel Green Bay to the playoffs with a win, Favre tossed three interceptions. It was the first of several poor performances in Minnesota.

9. Gift Pick for the Eagles

DATE: January 11, 2004
SCORE: Eagles 20, Packers 17
WHY IT MATTERED: Favre led Green Bay to a first-quarter advantage in this NFC playoff contest, then seemingly disappeared for the rest of the game. Handed a chance to win in overtime, Favre heaved an ill-advised pass into the hands of Philly's Brian Dawkins. The Eagles converted the pick into the game-winning field goal.

10. Forgettable Pro Debut

DATE: November 10, 1991
SCORE: Redskins 56, Falcons 17
WHY IT MATTERED: This game was actually Favre's second NFL appearance, but it was the first in which he threw a pass—four to be exact. Two were caught...both by Redskins. In fact, Favre's first NFL pass was intercepted and returned for a TD. Final passer rating: 0.0. It's amazing that he ever played again in the league.

Newly minted, 39-year-old Viking Brett Favre takes a breather during a preseason game against the Houston Texans on August 31, 2009, in Houston.

But I see myself as a Packer, and that's it. I don't ever see myself in another uniform. And when it's time, I hope I know."

I hate all of the talk about how huge the game on November 1 is going to be, when the Vikings play the Packers up on the frozen tundra of Lambeau Field. That is going to be the climactic crescendo in this whole soap opera. How many camera angles will there be for that "money shot" everybody wants to see—Favre running through the tunnel and out onto the field

> *"I see myself as a Packer, and that's it. I don't ever see myself in another uniform. And when it's time, I hope I know."*
> *—Brett Favre (2005)*

wearing a purple No. 4. They're saying it could be the most watched non–Super Bowl game in NFL history. I am sure the ratings will be through the roof. We'll see cheering, we'll see booing, it will be insane. And the hero-to-villain clichés are going to come at us in waves.

The rumors and craziness about it all still persist. There was even a report that came out that said the Favre family had secretly booked a big block of rooms at the Midway Motor Lodge Hotel in Green Bay early this summer, way before he had signed with the Vikings. Enough, already!

I do, however, love the promotional idea of WTDY Radio in Madison, donating unwanted Favre jerseys to the homeless. According to their website, Dan Deibert and Kurt Baron, the "Wisconsin Guys," are collecting Favre jerseys, hats, and sweatshirts as part of a "4 the Poor Jersey Drive." They say burning, shredding, and running over Favre gear are all "pretty good ideas." But they say a better idea is donating the "useless" clothes to a Twin Cities homeless shelter so they don't go to waste. That is awesome.

Last, but certainly not least, I hate all the Favre jokes about him being so damn old. Knock it off! Truth be told, the guy is exactly 118 days younger than I am, and I am starting to get a complex. If they keep saying that he's over the hill and washed up, then what the hell does that make me?

Okay, Here Is the Bottom, Bottom Line...

I love to hate Brett Favre and I love to love Brett Favre, in a bipolar, schizophrenic kind of way. I went from hating him up here in Minnesota to now loving him, while many Packers fans went from loving him to hating him. He is just such a polarizing figure, there is not much gray area in between. He truly is a love/hate kind of guy. As for now, I am just excited about the possibilities, about our chances this year with No. 4 leading the way. As I have mentioned ad nauseam, we need a Super Bowl and we need a new stadium, and if Brett Favre can help us accomplish those goals, then I will continue to love him. I am sure at the end of the day he will retire as a Packer and he will be inducted into their Ring of Honor. I hope so, he gave the organization a lot of good years and he deserves it. Not now, not for what he did in coming to Minnesota to get revenge (allegedly), but down the road, after he has been inducted into the Pro Football Hall of Fame and the wounds have healed.

> *I love the promotional idea of WTDY Radio in Madison, donating unwanted Favre jerseys to the homeless.*

I just hate not knowing for sure why he came back. That's the million-dollar question. Why? Does he want to try to humiliate Ted Thompson by crushing the Pack at Lambeau? Does he need the money? Does he need more fame and fortune? Does he truly want to win another Super Bowl? Does he want to win more awards? Why? The guy already has the awards and accolades, and he owns nearly every passing record in the book. So what else could possibly motivate him? Will his bionic arm still hold up at the age of 40? Will he be able to pull off the ultimate "screw you" on the biggest stage of his life? Stay tuned, it is going to be one hell of a wild ride!

ONE

Players Love to Hate Brett Favre

Jerry Kramer
Packers Hall of Fame Guard

Like most of the Packers faithful, I am not one bit happy about Brett signing with the Vikings. It was something that I don't think had to happen. I think because of maybe some egos in the Packers' head office, with Ted Thompson, it happened. It pissed Brett off, and I think he is a "by God, I'm gonna show 'em" kind of a guy, which only added fuel to the fire. As for why he chose to go to the Vikings of all places: from the way I see it, it's pretty simple—he's pissed. He felt like he was mistreated. A lot of this goes back to his feud with Ted over getting Randy Moss a few years back. Brett had Randy halfway talked into it, but Ted didn't pull the trigger for whatever the reason. Brett was all excited about that and, when it didn't happen, that was the beginning of the end, in my eyes. Can you believe that they thought a fourth-round draft pick was more valuable than Randy Moss? That was what it cost New England to get him; that's it. Unbelievable. Maybe Ted thought Moss couldn't behave himself up here after that whole mooning incident on *Monday Night Football* a few years back, who knows? Well, Brett was pissed about that because he wanted to get in another veteran receiver who he could lean on. The Packers had been going with a lot of younger players at that point, and he wanted to get some people in there who he thought could help the team win right now—because that is what Brett Favre is all about: winning. I am sure every time he saw Tom Brady hit Moss for a touchdown that season it got him madder and madder. Eventually he probably just snapped and said, "To hell with it."

All of that was the beginning of the feud with Ted, I suppose, but it got worse from there when he named Rodgers as his starting quarterback in, like, February that off-season. That was unheard of, naming your guy before training camp even opened. It rubbed a lot of people the wrong way, that was for sure. I am sure Brett saw that and said, "Wait a minute, I have been the quarterback for 17 damn years, haven't I got a little something coming here?" That probably wounded Brett even further and caused more hard feelings. So I think the reason Brett Favre is playing for the Vikings today is because of this. I really do. I am not inside his head and privy to everything, but I have talked to enough folks who know what's going on. I am not saying Brett is without fault on all of this, either. Lord knows he could have handled this differently, too. The guy can't make up his mind to save his life, we all know that. But overall I think the rift started over Moss and then came to a boil over Rodgers being named as the starter—basically telling him that the team had moved on without him.

> "When he walks onto the field at Lambeau Field wearing that purple jersey, it's gonna be nuts. Folks are gonna go whacko...it's gonna be a mess."
> —Jerry Kramer

As for how well Brett will do in Minnesota? Well, they have a hell of a team up there this year. I would say this, if Brett can somehow set his ego aside and just hand the ball off to Adrian [Peterson], they will probably go a long way. I don't know how far, but I think it will be far. His arm still looks really good, but with Brett you never know. If he lays low and hands it off to Adrian, they will be fine. But if he keeps trying to throw the son of a bitch into double coverage just because he can, then it's going to be a long year for him. That has always been his problem, always. Here is a stat to chew on, Bart [Starr] threw 244 passes in championships, playoffs, Super Bowls, and games to determine titles over his career. Do you know how many interceptions he threw in those games? One. You have to protect the ball, and that has always been Brett's Achilles' heel. He is such a tough competitor and he so badly wants to win that he will too often force balls into situations where they shouldn't be forced. You live with him and die with him that way, though. That is just all a part of the local lore and legend of the mighty Brett.

I will tell you this, though, when he walks onto the field at Lambeau Field wearing that purple jersey, it's gonna be nuts. Folks are gonna go whacko. They're gonna boo, they're gonna cheer, they're gonna cry; it's gonna be a mess. There are a lot of mixed emotions surrounding it. People have strong feelings one way or the other with him, and that only enhances all of this drama that is going on. A lot of folks are really down on him and are ready to hang him. They think he should have retired. Other folks still love him, and in their eyes he can do no wrong. So there is a wide variety of opinions out there right now.

I remember seeing Bart [Starr] at an autograph signing a couple of years ago, and we got to talking. There had been some rumblings in the media at the time about how maybe Brett had lost a step and that maybe it was time for him to finally hang it up. So I asked Bart what he thought about the situation. I said, "It looks to me like Brett is throwing the ball as well as he ever has, what do you think, Bart?" He looked at me and said, "Jerry, Brett throws the ball better on his knees today than I ever did standing." That says a lot in my opinion. There was still a lot left in the old tank at that point, and the Packers should have made every effort possible to get him back on the field.

As for whether or not they will ever retire Brett's number in Lambeau one day, I think it will happen eventually. I would hope they would, at least. I hope there is a little more class than that, to be honest. Most of the fans will forgive him down the road, but not all of them. Some of them will never get over it. They feel scorned and betrayed and nothing will ever change that. As for his legacy? I would say for starters you would have to look at his durability because he is as tough as they come, without a doubt. There has never been a question about his desire or love of the game, either. That is the biggest thing I think people will remember him for. No matter what the hell was hurting or aching, the guy always showed up to work. And after 18 seasons

> "It may require some whiskey, but yes, I will be rooting for Brett as a Viking—as much as that pains me."
> —Jerry Kramer

he is still going strong, unbelievable. What a story this kid is. Anyway, that is what I will remember about him. I will always remember those silly-ass underhanded, between-the-legs, behind-the-back, high school passes, too—because only Brett Favre could pull that off.

I will be honest, I am going to miss him in Green Bay. I am a hell of a Packer-backer, there is no question about that. But I am going to sneak a peak every once in a while over at No. 4 to see how he is doing. Call it a guilty pleasure or call it what you want, I just wish him well. Yes, I am going to pull for Brett every game this year, except for two. It may require some whiskey, but yes, I will be rooting for Brett as a Viking—as much as that pains me.

Joe Theismann
Hall of Fame Quarterback and Former Monday Night Football *TV Analyst*
I gotta be honest, Brett Favre doesn't look good in purple. He looks good in green and he should have stuck with that. Purple is reserved for one person in Minnesota, and that is Prince. My take on Brett going to the Vikings is this: it could turn out to be an okay year, it could turn out to be a dream season, or it could turn out to be a nightmare. I am leaning more toward the nightmare at this point, I really

am. Why? For starters, his missing training camp was a big deal in my eyes. Regardless of the whether or not he is already familiar with the system, the West Coast offense, that isn't as important as the continuity and

> *"Purple is reserved for one person in Minnesota, and that is Prince."*
> —Joe Theismann

chemistry that he needs to build with his receivers. Trust me, that stuff takes time and patience. As a result, he is learning on the fly. Throw in the fact that he just had surgery on his bicep and, oh, by the way, it turns out he has a tear in his rotator cuff. Those are some big ifs in my book, absolutely. And as far as the Vikings "letting him skip training camp," I say kudos to Brett. I begrudge the guy for absolutely nothing. If they are stupid enough to let him get away with stuff like that, then they are the ones who are fools. Hey, in life I think you ask for everything. Brett obviously didn't want to go, and his demands were met. Again, kudos.

From the way I see it, Brett has the potential to be the wick on a powder keg up there. Let's just say that he struggles, and there is a decent chance that he could, all hell could break loose. Look, last year the coaches in New York didn't have the guts to sit him down in order to try to save their season. That isn't going to happen in Minnesota. That team is too good. So I think Brad quite possibly could be faced with one of the most difficult decisions in football—and that is to tell

an icon that he has to take a seat. There was only one other player of that caliber that I have seen that happen to in recent history and that was Jerry Rice, when Mike Holmgren sat him down in Seattle. It was Jerry's last season in the league and it was unfortunate that he had to go out like that. Hall of Famers

> *"He has waffled back and forth so much, I am not sure he nows whether or not he wants to play himself. Today he does. What about tomorrow, though?"*
> —Joe Theismann

deserve better, but this is a young man's game. Mike was Jerry's first coach in San Francisco, so he knew him probably better than anybody. He was the one who had to say to him, "Jerry, you are kidding yourself." Would Brad Childress be able to have that same conversation with Brett should it come to that? Who knows?

Look, I have no problem with Brett Favre wanting to play as long as he can. But he has waffled back and forth so much, I am not sure he knows whether or not he wants to play himself. Today he does. What about tomorrow, though? He didn't want to play for the Jets after last season, so he convinced them that he was going to retire. As a result, they released him. Was that a ploy to get out of his contract? We will never know. But it worked, and as a result he got something that is very rare and very coveted in the world of professional football—unrestricted free agency. Very seldom does an athlete have a chance to call his own shots. As an unrestricted free agent, Brett was able to go to a place where the Packers wouldn't allow him to go a year before.

Do I think revenge was a factor in Brett going to Minnesota? Absolutely I do. Absolutely. Don't kid yourself. As passionate as we are about the game, there was always somebody that you wanted to be better than. There isn't a person out there that reads this book that didn't have somebody that they wanted to stick it to—whether it was the pretty girl sitting next to you in class who got all the attention, or the big jock who partied while you studied, or the coworker who got the promotion ahead of you. That is human nature. Inside all of us is that innate desire to stick it to the people that we feel wronged us. So for somebody to say that revenge is not a motivational factor in Brett's decision to join the Vikings, they're not only blind—they're stupid.

> "The body betrays you eventually, it happens to us all. That is sad, but that's life."
> —Joe Theismann

I have heard all the rumors, too, about the Vikings wanting to sign Favre so that they can get some traction as far as getting a new stadium. Hey, everybody uses everybody in this game. The Jets did it last year when they signed Favre, absolutely. Their signing of him was as big a ploy to sell tickets as I have ever seen. They used him. Without a doubt. Are the Vikings using him for that? Probably. The fact of the matter is that Brett is a huge draw, especially up there where the fans used to despise him when he was a Packer. So it is a great story, no question. As far as a stadium, though, I think that might take a Super Bowl or two. I gotta be honest. I don't know whether or not the Vikings are going to be able to keep that team in Minnesota. If they do move to L.A., however, it won't be for a while. That stadium is not going to be ready for at least a couple of years. Make no mistake, though, that group out there wants a team *badly*. And they are willing to do whatever it takes to get one. Who it will be remains to be seen, but the Vikings are certainly on the short list from the way I see it.

What makes Brett Favre so good is his durability. You have to be able to line up and play in order to accomplish anything in our game. When I talk to young quarterbacks, whether they are rookies in the NFL or youngsters, I tell them that the most important thing they can be is available to practice and play. With Brett, the guy has never missed a start. He plays through injuries and he plays hurt. He is so tough. I saw him play one time with a busted thumb on his throwing hand. They wanted him to sit out, but he insisted upon taping a tongue depressor to it instead. It was amazing to see him go out there and throw the ball like it was no big deal. I have to just marvel at his tolerance for pain. They guy is just a warrior.

Beyond that, what makes him such an endearing character is the fact that he has such a passion for the game. He is like a little kid out there just having fun. He is like Tom Sawyer and Huck Finn. He is also someone who people see as a real person. I mean, we have gone through the trials and tribulations of his life right alongside him. We were there when he lost his father; we were there when Deanna got cancer; we were there when he battled his addiction to drugs—the guy is real. What you see is what you get with Brett Favre.

You see so many players, the Pac Man Joneses and the Terrell Owenses of the world, who are great players but at times have been a disgrace to the game. Brett has been through his ups and downs over the years, but he is a good person and he has been good for football. The guy is a winner, and that is why so many millions of fans adore him. I don't know whether or not Brett Favre is the greatest quarterback ever to play the game, but I do know he is probably the greatest entertainer that has ever played that position.

> "Inside all of us is that innate desire to stick it to the people that we feel wronged us. So for somebody to say that revenge is not a motivational factor in Brett's decision to join the Vikings, they're not only blind—they're stupid."
> —Joe Theismann

Look, I am as big a Brett Favre fan as you are going to find. I've golfed with him and spent time with him, he is a great guy. But I don't think he has handled the last two years of his career very well for himself. While some people have become very resentful of the way he has gone about it, others are downright confused. Personally, I love him; but professionally, as a journalist, I am critical of him. At one time I said I thought he ought to retire. He proved me wrong. Will he prove me wrong again? I hope so. He still has the desire and passion, but I question his ability at this point, because of his age and his various ailments. It used to be that whenever Brett lined up under center, you couldn't count his team out. Not anymore. Not at the age of 40 and with all of his injuries. It's just not the same. The body betrays you eventually, it happens to us all. That is sad, but that's life. Hey, had I not gone through my career-ending injury [a broken leg], I probably would have been just like Brett, trying to play until I was 50. No doubt. Nobody wants to quit this game, this is all we know. We are football players. That's who we are. In my opinion, the ultimate reason why Brett Favre won't leave the game of football is the same reason Brett Favre is so great. This game means so much to him, and he doesn't want to give it up. Who would? It's the greatest game on earth.

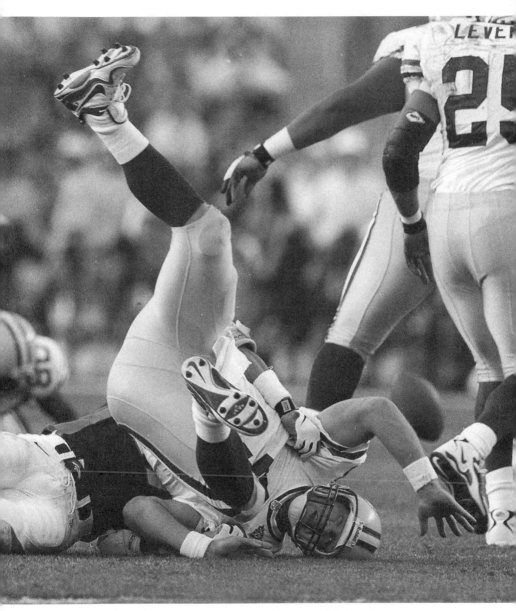

Brett Favre bites the turf after being sacked by Denver's Stever Atwater during the Packers' 31–24 loss to the Broncos in Super Bowl XXXII on January 25, 1998, in San Diego, California. *Photo courtesy of Getty Images*

Mark Chmura
Former Packers Tight End

On why he signed now: The only thing I can think is he knew this all along, and the only reason he delayed this is because he didn't want to go to camp. And I don't know why he doesn't want to go to camp because the quarterbacks have the easiest camp outside the kickers in the whole deal. This had to premeditated, especially with [Sage] Rosenfels playing so well this weekend, that they called Favre out of the blue and sent a jet down to pick him up and sign a contract.... I wish he stayed retired, I really do. You know, I love the guy to death, but enough is enough. You're tugging at Packers fans' heartstrings, and it's just time to let it go. Let it go.

On how the team will receive him: I think they [the Vikings] handled the whole [signing] situation very poorly. I would love to be in that locker room when he first arrives, cause there's clearly gonna be players in there that are not happy, and it's not just gonna be the two quarterbacks. You really form a bond with players in the off-season: in the weight room, spending time with them in the training room. So that's gotta be an awkward situation for Brett. I can't imagine he is so arrogant he's gonna walk into any situation, any locker room, and think everyone loves him. I think we saw that in the Jets locker room at the end of last year where he had players talking ill of him. It's gonna be interesting because if he does not start off very well and is being outplayed by these other two players, it could get very ugly.

On how quickly he'll get acclimated: The West Coast terminology is familiar all around the league, so for him to pick that up, it's gonna be very quick. He's just gotta get in football shape; I don't think he approached this off-season as if he was going to play. So the biggest thing for him is to get into playing shape; the shape that he's in right now, they throw him into a preseason game where he's gotta scramble, he's gonna pull something at close to 40 years old.

On the Brett Rules: Brett had his own set of rules. For instance, he didn't have to ride the bike down at training camp. He didn't have to go to certain events, they [the Packers] would shuffle him in to avoid the crowds. Those were kind of Brett's unwritten rules that the other guys didn't have to go through. Looking back, I think that Mike Sherman wrecked him. He just gave him the keys and let him do whatever he wanted to do, and that was what Brett expected to do from there on out. So that's why I am saying that there is going to be resentment in that Vikings locker room. It's all going to come down to Childress and how they run that organization, because if they let him change in his own locker room and have his own program, then this is going to be a huge distraction. They are going to go from a Super Bowl contender to an average team.

I think it all boils down to the fact that Brad Childress knows that he is on the hot seat. The only thing I can equate this to would be the Sterling Sharpe situation early in my career. In his own mind, he thought that he too deserved this type of treatment. It drove Holmgren nuts to the point where he wanted to get rid of him. In fact, I really believe that if Sterling hadn't hurt his neck, he would've been gone the next year, anyway. Those type of distractions can destroy a team. They really can. So if Brett goes out and plays very average and is outplayed by Sage Rosenfels or Tarvaris Jackson, you're going to see this team implode. It is a touchy situation. I just think that Minnesota handled the situation very poorly.

> *"I don't think people hate him so much because of the fact that he decided to come back and play, I think they dislike the fact that he is jerking everybody around."*
> *—Mark Chmura*

On Brett's legacy: I don't think people hate him so much because of the fact that he decided to come back and play, I think they dislike the fact that he is jerking everybody around, I mean he is jerking *everybody* around in this entire country. I don't think [Michael] Jordan was this bad. I can't think of any athlete who has retired and unretired this much. It's bad.

On indecision: Two weeks ago [prior to his signing] he said he couldn't play the game at the level he wanted to play at. What has changed in two weeks? I think that is what everyone is upset about—the history of that. Make a decision and stick with it. You know, I love Brett. I played with him for eight years, but he's driving me nuts.

On his reaction to Favre's signing: I just threw up in my mouth. Okay, this is what we found out. Brad Childress is a liar, the Vikings organization is a liar, Bus Cook is a liar, and Brett Favre is a liar. Now that's all right if you want to be a liar. That's fine. I don't have a problem with that. But the next time you are crying up at the podium, don't expect us to believe you. I have heard many people call up and say it's the media's fault, it's the media's fault. Well, it's not the media's fault, it's his fault.

> *"Okay, this is what we found out. Brad Childress is a liar, the Vikings organization is a liar, Bus Cook is a liar, and Brett Favre is a liar."*
> —Mark Chmura

On hearing the news that Brett signed with Minnesota: I was shocked because I believed him two weeks ago. You know, when a professional athlete says, "I can't do this anymore, my body won't allow me to play at this level, I don't have the drive, I cannot do it anymore," that's pretty much shutting the door. The first thing I would ask him is what happened in those two weeks where you can now play at this level? The guy is nuts! What can this guy do where you are going to believe him?

On a secret deal: This is how I think it went down. I think it was done about two months ago, and they all got together where Brett said, "I don't want to go to Mankato and have a roommate and live in a dorm. So how about I just come in for Week 2 or Week 3 of training camp?" I think that is how it went down. I think that Brad Childress is Mike Sherman in sheep's clothing. He is going to give Brett whatever he wants. He is going to give him his own locker room. He is going to let him throw his interceptions.

I don't think they are going to be as good as people think they are this year, either. I think he is going to make some boneheaded throws. Everyone's talking about how he has Adrian Peterson. Well, sure, but what I think defenses are going to do is load the box and say, "Look, let's get as many hits on Favre as we can." Then, if [the Vikings] decide to run the ball, [the defense is] already in good position to shut that down. It is tough to get everyone on the same page as far as blocking assignments when they [the opposition] are sending everyone at you [blitzing]. Look, the past four years after Weeks 8, 9, and 10, he has gone significantly downhill. So are people going to think that this is the year he is going to have 16 great games? I just don't think it happens. I think there is a pattern over these past four years where he is going to be great the first six games, he is going to be average over the next two or three, and then he is not going to be very good.

On revenge: Don't get me wrong, I love Brett. But these last couple of years it has gotten a little ridiculous. I mean, if you're going to tell me that you're not going to play for the Minnesota Vikings to stick it to the Packers, to stick it to Ted Thompson, and to stick it to the fans—then you're crazy. Crazy. Because no one would go into that situation, at least none of the guys who I played with. He had one focus in mind. Look, had the Patriots wanted him after Tom Brady blew his knee out, I still don't think Brett would have gone there. He wanted to go to Minnesota. It was all about sticking it to Ted Thompson. It was about, "This is my team. I used to own this team. How dare you get rid of me? I was Caesar and you were Brutus and Cassius."

Gilbert Brown
Former Packers Tackle
On hearing the news that Favre went to Minnesota: When I heard the news this morning, I thought, *Did Luke Skywalker go over to the Dark Side?* Seriously, grown men should never wear purple.... Hey, I want to come back and put on the pads one more time so I can get a hit on him. Back when we played [in practice], I never got to hit him because

he always had on that red jersey. Well, now that he is wearing purple, I want to get reinstated for just one game so I can finally get that hit on him that I have been waiting so long for!

On loyalty: Look, I am a loyal guy. Everybody knows that I took less money in order to stay with the team. For me, though, if the Packers had let me go and Minnesota told me that the door was open to sign there—for me—I wouldn't do it. It comes down to loyalty, and I come from the old school. The fans deserve to see their heroes stay put and to not change colors. It's just plain and simple. But if they do leave and have to change their colors, then they should not go to the colors of the team that their fans hate the most.

On whether or not his move to Minnesota was about sticking it to Ted Thompson: If I had to give you a percentage, I would say about 100 percent! Look, the fans have to understand—this isn't anything against them. They may say he is selfish or whatever because he is now in purple. But to me, this isn't about the fans, it's a vendetta between him and Ted Thompson, and the fans are caught in the middle of the whole thing. I am pretty sure he has mad respect for Aaron Rodgers, because he hasn't got anything to do with it.

Trent Dilfer

Former Pro Bowl Quarterback and ESPN Analyst

On retirement: Why? Brett has $12 million reasons why. I can tell you after being retired, this is a hard game to give up. I feel for anyone who has played in the NFL for an extended period of time who has to transition to the real world. It's scary. This is all we know, it is all we have been doing since we have been 10 years old. I completely understand why Brett can't give it up. However, I don't agree how he went about it. With Brett, you just can't love the way he plays football, this bipolar way of playing the game, and not expect it to translate it over to his real life. He is the same guy off the field as he is on the field. We love it on the field, but we can't stand it off the field. That's Brett.

On Packers fans hating Brett Favre: Look, I hate the Minnesota Vikings, too. I played for Tampa Bay in the old NFC [Central], the greatest division in football, and we hated those guys. I still have a hard time being objective when I evaluate the Vikings for those reasons. So I can understand why Packers fans just want to throw up with this move. But I don't know how you can hate Brett Favre. What he did for that organization, the legend that he is … why hate Brett Favre?

He simply wants to keep playing football. I don't know if there is an analogy I can use in the real world, but it is so ingrained into who he is. It is wound into his fabric as a human being. Why shouldn't he be able to keep playing? He couldn't play for the Packers anymore, so this is his decision. I don't think

> *"When I heard the news this morning, I thought,* Did Luke Skywalker go over to the Dark Side? *Seriously, grown men should never wear purple."*
> —Gilbert Brown

Packers fans should hate Brett Favre, but rather they should just continue to hate the Minnesota Vikings.

You cannot understand this unless you have done it and been an NFL quarterback. The reason why we go through what we go through, with the pain and the emotional tormenting that we endure, is because it is who we are. Now, if you take that away from us, it is brutal. It is a very hard transition. Players want to play this game for as long as they can. I remember playing with Jerry Rice at the end of his career in Seattle, and he was a shell of what he once was. I didn't hate him for coming back, though, because I could understand why he wanted to keep playing football—that is just who he is.

Cris Carter
Former Pro Bowl Vikings Wide Receiver

It's rare [for a franchise player to play for a rival], but I'm not shocked. There are a lot of guys who played a long time with franchises and might have ended [their careers] not on the best of terms, and they would love to go to a division rival. They would. There's more guys out there like that than you can imagine.

Rodney Harrison
Former Pro Bowl Patriots Safety
I don't think, personally, that Brett Favre is the answer. I think that move really came in and kind of sabotaged that locker room. I mean, you've got two guys, young quarterbacks, who were looking forward to competing for a starting job, and all of a sudden you get a guy and you pay him $12 million and you anoint him. He doesn't even come in and earn the position. He just comes in and he takes over. So I think he needs to come in, he needs to win the respect of that locker room, and the only way you do that is you go out there and make plays and you handle your business accordingly. But I don't think he's truly the answer. I don't think even with this move that Minnesota will get to the NFC championship, let alone the Super Bowl.

Nick Barnett
Packers Linebacker
I know you're looking for a good story, but I could absolutely give two [expletives] about it. Does it make it any more sweeter, Brett Favre playing for the Vikings? I don't know. I won't know until we're out there. Would I like to hit him? Hell, yeah, I'd like to hit him. All these damn practices out here and they didn't let us hit him? I want to get a nice little shot on you, Brett. I said it. Put it on the bulletin board.

> *"Hell, yeah, I'd like to hit him. All these damn practices out here and they didn't let us hit him? I want to get a nice little shot on you, Brett. I said it. Put it on the bulletin board."*
> *—Nick Barnett*

Al Harris
Packers Cornerback
We're going about our business. The fact is that he decided to play, he gets another chance to do what he loves to do, so I'm happy for him. But we're here, we're grinding, we're concentrating on what's happening in this locker room. We support Aaron. Aaron's our guy. No disrespect

to Brett—when Brett was here, he was our guy—but this is where we are right now.

Aaron Rodgers
Packers Quarterback
On whether Favre's ambiguity regarding retiring affects the Packers:
It does. How can it not affect it? I mean, when he flew into Green Bay the day after—or the day of the Family Night scrimmage, I mean that was ... talk about an awkward locker room. I mean, I've been the guy since March, you know? And then everybody's like, "Well, okay, what's gonna happen? Brett's gonna come back, he's gonna be the guy? Or Aaron's gonna be the guy? Or they'll compete for the job?" Nobody knowing what's going on—of course that's going to affect your football team.

As for our relationship? I mean, it was me and him. The last year, '07, we had no other quarterback on the roster. It was me and him, you know, we'd see each other every day, jog around with each other every day. You know, he knew how I felt about him, that I had the utmost amount of respect for him ... and to not have talked to him in over a year? That's disappointing.

John Randle
Former Vikings Pro Bowl Defensive End
I never thought in my wildest dreams that Brett Favre would be wearing purple. Never. I never would have even imagined it. No way. To see him go from being Minnesota's arch-nemesis to their hero, it is just so uncanny. Seeing all of these purple Favre jerseys up here in Minnesota, it's nuts. It still doesn't look right. Every time I see him on TV or in the paper, it's like I have to do a double-take. Man! We used to really get so pumped up to play that guy. I remember we would put his jersey on our tackle dummies and on the blocking sleds and stuff like that, so we could get the feeling of sacking him and hitting him. It was like a shark getting that first taste of blood. Now, though, he is one of us. How crazy is that?

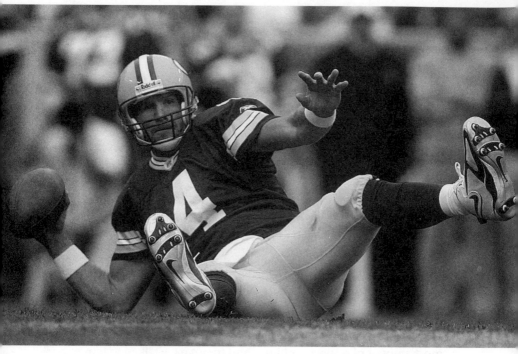

Favre looks to pass the ball after landing on his butt during a 26–0 loss to the Chicago Bears on September 10, 2006, in Green Bay.

For him to come here to Minnesota, Green Bay's biggest rival, there has to be more to it than people make. I don't know what went down between him and the Packers, but it must have been something pretty severe. I mean, to go from being a Packers icon to wanting to go to the enemy, they must have done something pretty damn serious to piss him off that much. I can honestly say that I would never have gone to play for the Packers at the end of my career. No way. I just couldn't do it. I know this is a business and all of that, but I have too much respect for the fans here. They gave me so much, and that would be like a stab in the back to do that to them. Now, I finished my career in Seattle, but that is totally different than Green Bay as far as rivalries go. Totally different. This rivalry, between Minnesota and Wisconsin, it's big time. These folks up here don't get along.

Everybody has their own conspiracy theory on why he left. Okay, here is mine: we all know the economy is down, so maybe the Packers wanted this all along as a sort of fundraiser? I mean, everybody in Wisconsin is throwing away their Favre jerseys now and buying Aaron Rodgers' instead. Hell, they are probably making millions right there!

Seriously, though, Brett is a great player, and I am happy for him that he is able to continue to play on his own terms. As players, we all want that. He is a hell of a quarterback, too—one tough SOB. I used to try to get under his skin all the time out there, and he made me work for everything I got, that was for sure. I was a trash-talker, so I was always trying to taunt him. Hell, he didn't care about that, though, he would just laugh. Shit, we would be talking back and forth across the line, saying all sorts of stuff at each other. It was awesome. I don't care what you would throw at him, though, he would always hold his ground. It was frustrating as hell from a defensive lineman's point of view. Eventually, when I couldn't rattle him, then I would start in on his linemen, to get them pissed off. That was Brett's Achilles' heel, his linemen, because they didn't know how to deal with that stuff and they would lose their cool. Once that happened, then I knew I could get to Brett. I got my hits on him eventually, I just had to be patient with that guy.

> "He knew how I felt about him...and to not have talked to him in over a year? That's disappointing."
> —Aaron Rodgers

Our rivalry got pretty intense and eventually Nike came to us about doing a commercial. [To play off their rivalry, Randle starred in a hilarious Nike commercial that featured him first sewing a miniature version of Favre's No. 4 jersey which he puts on a live chicken. The commercial then shows Randle in his Vikings uniform chasing the chicken around his backyard—as if he were practicing for the real thing. It then ends with Randle barbecuing the chicken on his grill, signifying the fact that he eventually got him!] That was a lot of fun, it really was. I later met Brett one time up in Chicago for a charity flag football game. We talked about the commercial, and he thought it was pretty funny. He is a good guy. Our rivalry on the field was pretty intense, but off the field we had a mutual respect for one another. We are both competitors and we both wanted to win.

I will tell you one rather interesting tidbit about that commercial, though. It aired for four years, and each of those four years I got audited by the state of Wisconsin. I don't know why, but they came after me hard. I never got audited from the state of Minnesota or even my home state of Texas, but Wisconsin always came looking for me. So I think the moral of the story here is: don't mess with Brett. Trust me, though, you don't want to mess with this guy—it'll cost you. In fact, from now on I may just refer to him as "Mr. Favre," just in case!

> "I can honestly say that I would never have gone to play for the Packers.... I have too much respect for the fans here.... That would be like a stab in the back."
> —John Randle

Bud Grant
Hall of Fame Vikings Coach

Players switch their allegiances pretty quickly these days, and that was unheard of when I was playing. Now, with free agency, it is like you have to check your team's roster every year to see who is on it. It used to be where players wanted to put down roots with a team, whereas nowadays that has all changed. The fans are pretty forgiving, too, of the players who leave and of those who come in. I mean, I was amazed at just how quickly Vikings fans embraced Brett Favre. Amazed. For an archrival to come here the way he did, and to see the fans here get behind him, it speaks volumes. Mostly, it speaks of the fact that the fans want their team to win. They don't care so much anymore about loyalty, they want to win. It is more superficial than I thought it was.

For me, as a coach, my job was to build a team and my approach was to build it with players who were going to be here. Sure, guys would come and go from year to year, but you would have the groundwork laid and then you just add pieces from there. Now, you can't do that anymore because there aren't enough players to build the groundwork. It is like a revolving door, some of these rosters nowadays. I can't keep up with it, I really can't. It's a whole new ballgame.

As for Brett not attending training camp, I didn't have a problem with that. Look, nobody enjoys training camp. None of us did. It's tough. When I was playing, I was late to every one of my training camps. I used any excuse I could find to get out of it. One year my wife was pregnant, which turned out to be a good one. Training camp is purgatory, it's not much fun. I think Brett is pretty smart, actually. He didn't want to be there and was able to come in on his own terms, so I say more power to him. I mean, in training camp, the quarterback throws *a lot*. The quarterbacks throw a ton of passes down there, and that is why teams bring in extra ones in order to help out. Well, Brett doesn't need all that needless wear and tear at this stage of his career. He's been to enough training camps, I think, to know what he can and cannot do. I'm sure the coaches weren't pleased, but that was the way it went. So I was okay with it, personally, but what do I know?

Look, training camp is not for everybody. I remember one year I excused [Hall of Fame defensive tackle] Alan Page from camp. Alan was a veteran and didn't care too much for training camp, so I let him take it off. He was a bright guy, and I trusted him to get into shape. The reality was that defensive linemen don't do a whole lot during that time other than bang around out there, so I let him take that time off to finish up his law degree, which was something he really wanted to do. The other players understood, and there wasn't any resentment toward him, I don't think, either. He was just a unique person. Everybody is unique in that way. Take a guy like [Pro Bowl running back] Bill Brown, he absolutely loved training camp. He loved the practices and he loved the banter with the guys—all the card games and hoopla. Some guys like it, they are away with the guys, away from their families for a few weeks, there are no distractions, no phone calls—for some it was like a vacation, believe it or not.

In my opinion, having Favre around would have made for an absolute media circus. Even all that was made about him out in New York last year with the Jets, where he supposedly had his own room within the locker room. Well, I am sure it was a logistical thing, not a prima donna thing. I mean, if you have 25 reporters in a locker room, 24 of them are probably going to be standing around Brett. I'm sure it wasn't so much about accommodating Brett as it was accommodating the rest of the players. Otherwise it is just a big distraction. People have no idea just how many reporters there are in New York, either; it is crazy out there. Plus, New York has a history of having open locker rooms—from the Yankees to the Jets and Giants. Well, as a coach I never understood that. I remember one time when [iconic TV analyst] Howard Cosell asked me why he couldn't come in our locker room. I said, "Howard, this is not New York. We don't allow reporters in here." He said, "What the hell are you talking about? I have always been able to go in the locker room, hell, I'm a locker room guy." I just smiled and said, "Howard, you're not a locker room guy in this locker room." He didn't care too much for that, but I didn't give a damn. I didn't want all that stuff in there, no way.

I have never met Brett Favre, so I can't comment on him as a person. But as a player, I think he is just an outstanding quarterback. His durability is the thing that really stands out in my eyes. I mean, the guy has never missed a start. What else can you say about the guy? You cannot achieve greatness without durability. No way. So I would say that durability is Brett's best ability. Bar none. Some guys just don't get hurt—for whatever the reason their bodies respond differently. They bend, whereas other guys will break. One week a guy will be out with a pulled muscle and the next week he will be out with a sore shoulder. From all my years in the league, I have realized that guys who get hurt tend to keep getting hurt. I don't know why, but it happens more often than not. So guys who are extremely durable in this league are special, valuable players—they are rare. Brett Favre is definitely a rare player, that is for sure.

Jerry Glanville
Favre's Former Head Coach with the Atlanta Falcons

We had Brett when he was a rookie, and you could see that he was a great competitor. Things didn't work out between us, though, and we had to part ways. Things didn't really work out. I don't want to get into all of it, but looking back I think Brett had some growing up to do at that point in his career. There were some things that happened, but nothing that I can share for the book or put into print. I'll let him tell it instead if he so chooses. I have never told the story of what happened, and by league rules I still can't talk about it. Therefore I won't.

As far as him not wearing the Packers green and gold anymore, I could care less—it doesn't bother me a bit. I will say this, though: I am coaching right now up in Portland State [Oregon] and we are the Vikings. Well, when I read in the paper this past August that he had signed with the Vikings, I got all excited. Then, when I learned it was those "other" Vikings, I settled down. I was hoping he might get confused and report here instead, but it didn't happen.

> "Brett had some growing up to do at that point in his career. There were some things that happened, but nothing that I can share for the book or put into print."
> —Jerry Glanville

Seriously, though, in retrospect, I am glad that Brett was able to go to Green Bay and be successful. Now that he is in Minnesota, I am sure he will do just fine. Like I said, he is a heck of a competitor.

Ahmad Rashad
Former Pro Bowl Vikings Wide Receiver

He just looks weird wearing purple. To me, Brett Favre will always be a Green Bay Packer. It would be like Magic Johnson wearing a green Celtics jersey, or Larry Bird wearing a gold Lakers jersey—either way, it's just wrong. Times have certainly changed, though. A signing like this *never* would have gone down when I played in Minnesota, never. Bud [Grant] never would have allowed the star of our rival team to jump ship like that. No way. It's a whole new world now, though, and there is not much loyalty anymore. That's for sure.

As for his signing, I am skeptical, I really am. I live in New York and I watched Brett last season. They had a legitimate chance to go to the Super Bowl, and their weak link, believe it or not, was at quarterback—especially in the second half, and that is when the season really starts in my mind. Sure, I know he was hurt, but he looked awful. So I am leery of how well he will do in Minnesota and if his body can even hold up. I know he had surgery on his arm this off-season, but from what I understand, he has some serious shoulder problems, too. I mean, the guy is 40, so I don't know. This was a pretty big gamble by the Vikings, in my eyes. The bottom line is this: if the players accept him and genuinely want him in the locker room and on the field, then it has a chance to work out—because those are the only opinions that matter in this game. If they embrace him and want to go to war with him and think that he can lead them to a Super Bowl, then there's hope.

> "I will eventually forgive him, even though he is an ass for signing with the Vikings."
> —Fuzzy Thurston

The thing is, in professional football nobody wants a retread. Your reputation means absolutely nothing in this game. It's all about "what can you do for me now?" Nobody cares about how many touchdowns you've thrown in the past 18 years, it's all about *right now* in this league. You threw 50 touchdowns last year? Great. How many are you going to throw this year? That is how fast this game moves, it is all about *right now*. This is a tough game played by young people. So it ain't gonna be easy for him, that much I know for sure.

Look, I've met Brett, and he's a nice enough guy. I wish him all the best, I really do. I admire him, too, for giving it a shot. He has been

Favre takes a seat after fumbling the ball away to the Falcons late in a wild-card playoff game on January 4, 2003, at Lambeau Field. The Falcons won 27–7.

great in this league, but greatness is as it *is*, not as it *was*. So if he pans out and leads them to the Super Bowl, then kudos Minnesota, that was a great move signing Brett Favre. I will be in Miami rooting you on, *Go Purple!* You know what, if Brett can come out of retirement to play up there, maybe they will re-sign me, too? Can you imagine that? I can hear it now: "Favre drops back and throws it deep … and it's caught by Rashad in the end zone, *touchdown Minnesota Vikings!*" How great would that be? Watch out Minnesota, I'm coming back!

Fuzzy Thurston
Former Packers Guard and Owner of Titletown Tickets and
Fuzzy's 63 Bar and Grill in Green Bay

As for Brett playing for the Vikings, I think it's terrible. I hate the Vikings even worse than the Bears—and that's a *big* hate. I am just very, very disappointed. I will always love Brett because nobody ever played their heart out more for the Packers than he did. He is the best football player I ever saw play for Green Bay. We had so many miserable years before Brett got here, and he helped to turn this franchise around. And he did it in such a big, big way. For that we will always be grateful. As for how I am going to feel when I see Brett run out onto Lambeau Field wearing a purple jersey, I am going to be so hurt and disappointed. I just never in my wildest dreams ever thought I would see Brett wearing a Vikings uniform. I would honestly rather see him as a Chicago Bear than as a Viking, and I really hate the Bears—just not as much as the Vikings. I will eventually forgive him, even though he is an ass for signing with the Vikings.

Troy Brown
Former Patriots Wide Receiver

If this team is winning, everybody will forget about what happened. But trust me, if they come out and lose the first couple of games, and they're not doing so well at the halfway point, and if they lose to Green Bay—God forbid they lose to Green Bay—it will be a fallout within that organization that you've never seen before.

Mark Schlereth
Former Denver Broncos Pro Bowl Guard and
Current ESPN Football Analyst

I know for a fact there are players in that locker room who don't trust him. They will say the right things, because they're pros, but you can't tell me that guys in that locker room don't feel, to some degree, betrayed.

The Media Love to Hate Brett Favre

Dave Sinykin
Longtime Host of The Packer Preview *Radio Show*

The word that comes to mind right away for most Packers fans is "disappointing." We all wanted the fairytale, storybook ending, and it, unfortunately, didn't work out that way. Brett is this incredible, almost-never-seen-before kind of quarterback that comes around maybe once in a lifetime. He sets all the records, brings home the trophy, and—oh, by the way—never takes a day off. It was unbelievable. Take all that and add it to the fact that he did it all in Green Bay, a franchise that had been way down for 25 years before he came, and he comes riding in on his white horse and almost single-handedly resurrects it. It was sort of like the Hebrews going through the Egyptian desert for 40 years, that was what it felt like for Packers fans. He then took us on this incredible 16-year run, where football was fun again. Here we are, the smallest market in the league, a team owned by the fans—literally—and *our* guy is the face of the NFL. In Green Bay, they live and die with that team; that is all there is up there. So as a fan you look at all of that and you figure that he is supposed to retire as a

Packer and then have his number hung up on the wall, like all of the other greats before him. Well, when that didn't quite work out, we were all pretty disappointed.

What takes it from disappointment to anger for a lot of fans, however, was just the way he manipulated his presence over the past few years. He retired in 2007 and then changed his mind. And then the team had to trade him because they knew that he wanted to sign with their biggest rival. That was sad in a lot of people's eyes. For me, personally, I was 100 percent behind the organization for sticking to their guns and going with Aaron Rodgers. They weren't going to let Brett hold them hostage, and I applaud them for that. I know they took a lot of heat for it, but I think in the end they are better off. I really do.

> "The fact that the majority of Vikings fans could just flip a switch and start loving him up makes me sick."
> —Dave Sinykin

As for him orchestrating the move to Minnesota, we have some serious trust issues with Brett. Once things went south, we knew that he wanted to come here all along. In fact, I don't believe he would be playing in the league this year for any team *but* Minnesota. I mean, if the Redskins had a similar offense and were in contention, I don't think for a second he would have gone to Washington. No way. He wanted to come here so that he could stick it to [Packers GM] Ted Thompson. The whole thing just smacks of revenge. But, hey, the stars aligned for him, and he is a Minnesota Viking. What are you going to do? It was really odd seeing that first purple No. 4 jersey, though, really odd. Almost surreal.

As for my personal theories on why he chose to come play for the enemy? Well, certainly some of it goes back to Randy Moss. It was no secret that Brett wanted Ted to sign him. The Packers had the youngest team in the league at the time, and Brett really wanted some veteran players who could help him out. I don't think Brett wanted to play his last few years with a bunch of kids. I look at that and say, "Hey, the game is bigger than you, Brett." They still had a great year in 2007, his last season in Green Bay, going 13–3. They nearly made it to the Super Bowl were it not for his, oh yeah, *interception* in overtime, which still really bothers me to this day—but I digress. The bottom line for me was that Brett didn't get his way and he pouted. Again, kudos to Ted for not caving in to him.

There are a lot of Vikings fans who are just sickened by the idea of Brett Favre wearing purple. In their eyes, he was the enemy for 16 years, and they simply cannot let that go. I get that. For me, it is kind of like when the Packers won the Super Bowl in 1997 with Jim McMahon as the backup to Favre. It bugs me to this day that he can walk around with a Packers Super Bowl ring, it really does. For me he was enemy No. 1 of the hated Bears; I can't stand that guy. Anyway, the thing that really bugs me is how so many Vikings fans immediately jumped on the Favre bandwagon and started rooting for this guy. I went to the first preseason game against the Chiefs, which was just a few days after he signed, and I couldn't believe how many purple Favre jerseys I saw. It was amazing. So the fact that the majority of Vikings fans could just flip a switch and start loving him up makes me sick. I am just not wired that way. If he is my rival, then I am never going to cheer for him. That is just me. Hey, I respect the Vikings fans who are saying, "You know what, I don't want to win a Super Bowl with this guy. I don't want Packers fans to say the only reason we won a Super Bowl was because it was with *our* guy."

Truth be told, I am pretty upset about it. Selfishly, I suppose, Brett is supposed to be *our* guy. My guy. I don't want to share him. Brett was my favorite Packer for a lot of years and now he is playing for the enemy. I was there in '97 when he led my team to the Super Bowl, and that was a special time for me, it really was. As much as I am mad at him, though, I have to just be grateful for the memories. Hey, as mad as I am at him, he is the reason I have a Packers show on the flagship radio station of the Minnesota Vikings. How unique is that? There are a ton of Packers fans in Minnesota, and I have been fortunate enough to be their voice, which is kind of neat.

As for therapy, I have been dealing with it in my own personal way. I took a golf club to my Brett bobble-head doll, and I am going to be hosting a Packers party the day before the *Monday Night Football* game [between the Vikings and Packers] at a local bar where I am going to invite fans to throw their Favre Packers jerseys into a wood chipper. It will be like that scene from the movie *Fargo*! It is going to be pretty funny, I can't wait.

I truly believe that the honeymoon for Vikings fans is now, though. I don't think there is any way he holds up the entire season without being injured. No way. With the off-season surgery, skipping training camp, his 40th birthday, and the shoulder problems—I think the streak comes to a halt sometime this season. I really do. So enjoy it while it lasts, Minnesota... enjoy it while it lasts. Then, when he goes down and ruins their season, they are going to hate him all over again. That is when the Packers fans will feel vindicated. In the end, I like our chances this year in Green Bay. We have a great young team and a very good quarterback in Aaron Rodgers. And thank goodness he is who he is, because if he was just a mediocre player, I don't know if Ted Thompson's life would be safe this year if Favre somehow wills Minnesota to the Super Bowl. Go Pack!

Bill Johnson
Sports Talk Radio Host, ESPN Milwaukee

The entire situation is pretty crazy. I mean, here is a guy who could have run for governor of Wisconsin and probably won. He was just that popular and beloved. Now, however, everything has changed. It is an incredible story, it really is. We have gone through all of this before, the drama with Brett, so we are used to it. We are kind of numb to it, to be honest.

I guess the million-dollar question is: why did Brett go to the Vikings? To me, I think it all starts and stops with Packers GM Ted Thompson. As much as Vikings fans and Packers fans hate each other, take that times 100 and that is how much Brett Favre doesn't like Ted. I don't get it, either. Even after he told [NFL commissioner] Roger

Goodell that he was out to get Ted; and even though he said last year when he went to the Jets that he came back for the wrong reasons; all of a sudden now Brett says he doesn't have a vendetta against Ted. I just don't understand it. Where that rift between the two of them started is debatable, but the fact remains that Brett definitely has some bile for him. So I think that has been what has driven him to this decision to come back and play for the Packer's greatest rival.

I think the feud started when Ted actually started telling Brett no. Nobody had said no to Brett since the Wolf-Holmgren era,

> *"Enjoy it while it lasts, Minnesota...enjoy it while it lasts. Then, when he goes down and ruins their season, they are going to hate him all over again."*
> —*Dave Sinykin*

and he didn't want to hear that. Brett had kind of been acting like he was the general manager of the team at that point, which had gotten out of control. Things heated up between the two of them when the team decided not to re-sign [offensive linemen] Marco Rivera and Mike Wahle. From there, I think Brett got upset about the fact that they didn't give Steve Mariucci an interview for the head-coaching job and instead gave it to Mike McCarthy. Another big thing that inflamed Brett was when the team drafted Aaron Rodgers with a first-round pick. Brett would have much rather the team have used that pick on someone who could help *him*, versus someone who was eventually going to take his job. The reality is that getting Aaron with the 24th pick of the first round was an absolute steal. They *had* to take him there. Then perhaps the straw that broke the camel's back was when Brett wanted Ted to sign Randy Moss, and [Moss] instead went to New England.

As for his much-anticipated return to Lambeau Field as a Viking? I just hope that there are more cheers than boos, I really do. I have been one of Brett's harshest critics since he left, but booing Brett Favre to me would be such an abomination, in my eyes. I'm sorry, but I think it's morally wrong to boo Brett Favre at Lambeau Field. I really do. I grew up in Wisconsin and have been a Packers fan my whole life, and I think this is one of those things you just don't do. Those are hallowed grounds. I never imagined in my wildest dreams that he would get booed at Lambeau, but I am sure it will happen. Look, I don't agree with what Brett Favre did, and I think fans have all the right in the world to be upset with him, but I just don't think it is the right thing to do to boo him at Lambeau. We shouldn't lower ourselves to that.

As for Brett's legacy? While a lot of Packers fans feel betrayed by him, there are still a lot of fans who are going to be undyingly loyal to him. I don't get it. Hearing Brett talk now, I gotta be honest, I never thought that he would be that small. I have worked in the media for a while, so I understand that the gild is off the lily as far as athletes being heroes, but I was shocked at how petty he came across in this whole thing. Yes, Brett served this organization well, *but* the organization and the fans treated him well, too. Then all he wanted to do when he had a disagreement with his boss was to go and play for their worst rival. That is just really, really petty as far as I am concerned.

As crazy as this whole thing has been, I think the Packers have been the "adult in this relationship," to tell you the truth. Brett has taken shots through intermediaries, the folks who I like to refer to as "sucking off the No. 4 teat," which would include the agent, the idiot brother, the long-suffering wife, the mother, and the various other family members down there in Mississippi. They take shots that he wants to take at the Packers. The organization knows though that eventually they are going to have to sell Brett Favre the Product all over again. That's why the Packers don't go out and tear him by saying stupid things. They know better. They know that eventually he will be back. The fact of the matter is that years down the road, after Brett is inducted into the Hall of Fame, he will come back to be inducted into the Ring of Honor. You can count on it. In fact, I wouldn't be surprised if they give him the same multimillion dollar marketing deal that they offered him prior to him going to the Jets. Crazy. I guess time heals all wounds.

D'oh! Another costly Brett Favre interception leads to a Packers defeat, this time in Super Bowl XXXII, on their way to a 31–24 loss to the Denver Broncos.

Steve "the Homer" True

Sports Talk Radio Host, ESPN Milwaukee

The whole thing makes me sick, to be honest. I have been very tough on Brett since day one. I think he is brilliantly manipulative and he has basically thrown everybody under the bus for his own personal whim. I don't think money is a big factor in this whole equation, but I'm sure it is to his agent. Regardless, he opted out, and his legacy will forever be tainted. Brett Favre has no loyalty. None. It's all about Brett.

Everybody owes Brett, he doesn't owe anybody anything. Look, Brett Favre is a very, very smart individual. This notion of him being this country bumpkin is a joke. As such, any premise that suggests Brett is not fully aware of what's going on around him is the biggest flaw most people make. It's not like he can't make up his mind or that he doesn't know what he's doing. He knows. The guy is a master manipulator. Look how he has used the media by leaking stuff to ESPN this past year or so. The guy is no dummy. It is just an amazing ruse that he's used for his own benefit to go about getting everything that he wants. What has Brett Favre ever wanted that he didn't get? It's a nice story for people to think that he can't make up his mind, but it's all a fabricated lie. Hell, I think if he was healthy that he would play until he was 50. What else is he going to do, sit on his tractor?

In my eyes, Brett Favre is [Boston Red Sox pitcher] Roger Clemens. He believes he can do whatever he wants, whenever he wants. He's selfish, and I think his behavior off the field is despicable. He has lied to his best friends. Just like Clemens, I don't think he has any real concept of what the truth is anymore. I had someone close to the Vikings tell me last year that they knew Brett was lying whenever his lips were moving. How ironic is that? All of that doesn't matter, though, because the players love to play with him. They know he can win, and that is the number-one thing for them. The reason he is as aggressive as he is on the football field is because he knows exactly where everybody is supposed to be. That confidence, along with the strength of his arm, makes him believe that he can do anything—and in many cases he has. I mean, the guy is a great quarterback, you can't argue with that. There has been a legitimate debate as far as his greatness as a player, though. I have always said that he and John

> "I think he is brilliantly manipulative and he has basically thrown everybody under the bus for his own personal whim.... His legacy will forever be tainted."
> —Steve "the Homer" True

Elway are probably the greatest regular-season quarterbacks ever. But as far as the postseason, he is nowhere near the quarterback that Bart Starr was. In fact, many would argue that Starr is in fact the best quarterback to ever play for the Packers.

When it first happened, everybody just assumed that the Packers just pushed him out. Now, as they get to see his true colors, they have come around more to side with the Packers, and not with Brett. It also helps that Aaron Rodgers is playing well, too, but that is another story.

At the end of the day, this is really personal to a lot of people. There is a great line in the movie *Hoosiers* where the outgoing Hickory coach [Chelcie Ross's character, George] says to the new coach [Gene Hackman's character, Norman Dale],

> "They thought he was Mr. Packer, but in the end they realized that he was just a liar."
> —Steve "the Homer" True

"Look, mister, there's two kinds of dumb: the guy that gets naked and runs out in the snow and barks at the moon, and the guy who does the same thing in my living room. First one don't matter, the second one you're kinda forced to deal with." Well, that's kind of what happened with Brett and the Packers. Eventually Ted Thompson said that they were going to have to move on, so they did. Brett couldn't handle that, though, so he pouted and got it all turned around so that Ted was the bad guy.

He told a teammate while all of this stuff was going on this past summer that his going to the Vikings was all a lie, that there was no truth to it. How can you do that? How can you lie to your friend like that? He has no concept of what the truth is anymore. I will say this, though: in everything he says there is an element of truth. But it is fundamentally a lie. It is like dealing with a teenager. After a while, you just have to shake your head and go, "Yeah...right." Even now, he says he may not play all 16 games this season for Minnesota. Well, that is to convince everyone that he is a "team guy" and that the consecutive-starts record isn't very important to him. What a crock, the record is *extremely* important to him, otherwise he wouldn't be going through all of this. No way. He wants to sell that load of bull to his teammates about how "it's all about the team" and not about him, and I'm sure they're buying it. Why wouldn't they? It sounds good, I'm sure.

So many people are so upset with Brett because it turned out he wasn't who they all thought he was. They thought he was Mr. Packer, but in the end they realized that he was just a liar. Playing for the Packers was of no significance to him. It was just a team he played for. I have to laugh when I think of his quote about his legacy, where he said, "If you're true Packers fans, you understand." I mean, how could anybody be so obtuse? Like, if they were "real" Packers fans then they would forgive him or something. What a crock. His point is that what he did was so great for this team that everybody is beholden forever. So—*what?*—he can do anything? In reality, there is nothing he could do on a negative that would equal all the positives. And again, classic Brett Favre, fundamentally there is some truth to that. Right? Doesn't everybody owe him for being entertained by him for so long? Apparently so. But to think on principal that he can do anything and then be forgiven, it's like: what world are you living in? Come on. Why not just say to the Packers fans something like this: "I am sure people are upset, and I apologize to them. I had to do what I felt was best. I understand that people are mad, and hopefully one day they will forgive me." Isn't that what a normal person would say? That's what makes this so bizarre. No one really knew that he was like this. Gosh, what a huge disappointment he turned out to be.

As for him coming back to Lambeau Field, it's going to be a mixed bag—some of the fans will cheer for him, and some will boo him. The majority of people have sided with him, but I think his behavior since then and all of the things that he has done have made people realize that he's nuts. This is Brett Favre, a player who people adored, going to play for the enemy. How would Bears fans feel if Walter Payton finished his career as the starting running back for the Packers? It's not like when Jim McMahon came to the Packers as a washed up backup after playing with the Bears, either. He was just basically wearing a uniform and holding a clipboard at that point, so it wasn't a big deal. For Brett to concoct a scheme to go to Minnesota, however, is totally different, in my eyes. I think in recent years the Vikings are Green Bay's No. 1 rival, absolutely. It used to be Chicago, but now it's definitely Minnesota. Look, he'll eventually be inducted into the Packers' Ring of Honor, and deservedly so for what he accomplished *on* the field. As for the fans forgiving him, though, I think most will ultimately forgive but they will never forget. Packer fans *never* forget. Regardless of what happens, the perception of Brett Favre will just never be the same. His image is tarnished. He showed us no loyalty; he left us. It's like God is now with the devil.

Even watching Childress pick up Brett at the airport, that is a huge deal to him—that's the kind of stuff he likes. Then with the helicopters and whatnot, it was so over the top. I mean, how many head coaches in the National Football League pick up their players at the airport? This is Brett's way of letting everybody know who is running the show. This isn't Childress' team, it's Brett's team. You'll see, just give it time. He's been calling the shots up there for months, and it will only continue. His true colors will eventually come out, I guarantee it.

Paul Charchian
Twin Cities Sports Talk Radio Host and Fantasy-Football Guru
From a fantasy-football perspective, Brett Favre has always been a big deal. There are nearly 30 million fantasy players in the U.S. and Canada, and all of them are affected by Brett's decision to come back. So his constant retiring and unretiring has definitely caused us some grief over the years....

Brett Favre's fantasy value has always swung wildly. Depending on your scoring system, and specifically how much interceptions hurt you, his value throughout the years has been tremendously varied. In fact, there were a lot of games where he scored negative points because of all the interceptions he threw. And that is just the nature of Brett Favre, you live with him and you die with him. He may throw five touchdowns, but he may also throw three picks—you just never know what you are going to get with him. That is the X factor with him, and that all goes back to his "gunslinger" mentality of always trying to force balls to make plays. ...

As for the big homecoming back in Green Bay when Brett runs out onto Lambeau Field, I think it will be five minutes of a lot of vitriol toward Brett and then it will just be about the Vikings and Packers playing football. I don't think it will be nearly as meaningful to Brett as it will be to the fans. It is going to be a lot harder on the fans than it will be for him, no question. Yes, a lot of disgruntled Packers fans have conspiracy theories on why he came back and about how he is going to exact revenge, but I think it is all a bunch of B.S. The Packers fans firmly believe that Brett can't get over the Packers, and they like the thought of this all being about them. ... If the fans want to be mad at anybody, they should direct their anger at Packers management, who, for whatever the reason, were unable to sign him two years ago. Move on people, get over it!

> "He may throw five touchdowns, but he may also throw three picks—you just never know...with him."
> —Paul Charchian

The rivalry here between Minnesota and Wisconsin is pretty intense, and adding Brett Favre to the mix just makes it even more combustible. He is such a polarizing figure to people, everyone just has a really strong opinion of the guy one way or the other—but there is nothing in between. I remember being on-air when Favre retired for the first time with the Packers. I remember the phone lines just lit up with nothing but thrilled Vikings fans who wanted to rub it in to Packers fans. We even played the song "Ding Dong the Witch is Dead" from *The Wizard of Oz*. It was pretty funny. At that point it had seemed as if 16 years of torture for Vikings fans was finally coming to an end. There was a huge sense of relief in the air, it was surreal. The burden had been lifted, in their eyes. Packers fans eventually started calling in, too, and the rationalizing started in from there: "Oh, we'll be better off without him...," "He was too old...," and, "Aaron Rodgers is way better, anyway...." Needless to say, it was hilarious. Ah yes, Brett Favre and sports talk radio—a match truly made in heaven.

Jim Souhan
Longtime Columnist for the Star Tribune

I love him and I hate him. I know it's a John Madden cliché, about how he just loves the game, but it's great to see someone play with that kind of enthusiasm. Say what you want, but the guy is a great player, truly magnetic. But I hate the fact that, even though he talks about how much of a team guy he is, at the end of the day we all know it's really just about him. He pretends to make it all about the team, but it's always been all about Brett. I don't know if I have ever had more conflicting opinions about one individual than I have about Brett Favre. I mean, he's an icon, he's a great player, he's a diva, and he's a mess. He might save this franchise and help us build a stadium, and he might ruin their season. He has left two teams in his wake, complaining about him as he left the door, yet the Vikings couldn't wait to get him in their door. So they know what they are getting in this guy, it's pretty obvious. Brad Childress basically had to sell his soul in terms of work ethic and commitment to training camp to get him to come in. But when you are desperate, I suppose you will do anything. So do I think it is all going to work? I don't know. Probably not, but who knows? Can a 40-year-old quarterback with an injured arm last an entire season and accomplish what they want him to accomplish? I doubt it, but it's going to make one hell of a story along the way. I mean, this is such a fascinating story, you just have to root for the guy.

Gene Wojciechowski
Sports Columnist, ESPN

It's a win for the Vikings: they get an experienced, Hall of Fame quarterback who is familiar with the division and intimately familiar with his former franchise, which just so happens to play in that same division. It's a win for Favre: he gets a playoff-caliber team, a potential Hall of Fame running back [Adrian Peterson], a killer offensive line, an offensive system he knows by memory, a speedy X factor in Percy Harvin, a domed stadium in the dead of winter, and another chance to play. It's a loss for the Packers, who were hoping Favre would simply go back to Mississippi and stay there.

Mike Florio
Sports Columnist, Sporting News *and ProFootballTalk.com*

I once believed quarterback Brett Favre was simply a victim of his ever-shifting mindset and emotions. But after watching at least a dozen times the clip of Favre saying in February 2009 that he definitely will not play again, I'm prepared to conclude that Favre's arrival in Minnesota was far more about calculation than serendipity.

In February Favre laid the foundation to secure a free-and-clear release from the Jets. When he got what he wanted in April, Favre said it had nothing to do with any desire to play for the Vikings. Momentum continued to build in that direction until, all of a sudden, Favre told Vikings coach Brad Childress (whom Favre calls "Chilly") that the Second Annual Retirement would not become the Second Annual Unretirement. The powers-that-be would have us all believe Chilly accepted Favre's decision without any effort to change his mind. Then Chilly ignored Favre for 20 days, and Favre ignored Childress for 20 days. But Chilly supposedly called Favre on Monday on a whim. And Favre—who agonizes over every decision in his life—instantly determined without deliberation or debate to re-retire from retirement and relocate to Minnesota for six months.

Think about that for a second. The guy who has dragged his feet in each of the past five off-seasons, waffling and wavering and waxing before deciding to play football again, suddenly decided in one day, based on one conversation, to commit to playing for the Vikings for an entire season. He didn't just fly to Minnesota to hammer out a contract. He came, he saw, he practiced. All in one day. And he'll play in a game [three nights later]. The whole thing would make far more—

but not complete—sense if Chilly and Favre would admit they talked over the past three weeks regarding scenarios in which Favre would ride in on a white plane and save the Vikings' season—and in turn, Chilly's job. So at a minimum Favre spent the past three weeks continuing to revisit the decision with Chilly and finally deciding after three weeks of additional deliberation and decision-making and -unmaking to go ahead and give it a shot. The more likely explanation is that it was all a ruse.... Lying is a way of life in the NFL, and Favre's presence in Minnesota is proof that we've all been lied to...again.

Jeff Pearlman
Sports Columnist, Sports Illustrated
Brett Favre has officially tossed his legacy down the toilet. A dark moment, it is. For the low, low price of a reported $12 million, Favre has officially and irrevocably morphed his reputation, going from greatest quarterback of all time to craziest sports egomaniac we've ever seen—and that includes Michael Jordan, Will Clark, Wilt Chamberlain, Roger Clemens, Barry Bonds. Truly, it's a head-spinning thing. In America, we love comebacks. Absolutely, positively eat them up. Jordan mothballs his White Sox uniform to return to the Bulls— we go bananas. Lance Armstrong dusts off his Huffy to give it another shot—we're all in his corner. Heck, it doesn't even matter how ill-advised or ill-fated the returns are. Does anyone really recall Jordan as a Washington Wizard? Or Sugar Ray Leonard having his face re-sculptured by Macho Camacho? Or Jim Palmer getting lit up in spring training at 45? Come back, old friends. Feel free. But this...this is different. In signing with (of all teams) the Minnesota Vikings, Favre is flashing a very large, very pronounced middle finger toward

> *"Favre has officially and irrevocably morphed his reputation, going from greatest quarterback of all time to craziest sports egomaniac we've ever seen."*
> —Jeff Pearlman

Green Bay, where his most loyal fans once resided. Even with last year's sorrowful run in New York, Favre was still assured a place alongside Vince Lombardi, Bart Starr, Jim Taylor, among the city's all-time gods. Now, however, he is Wisconsin's own Benedict Arnold—a cheese-hating, beer-gagging, bratwurst-regurgitating foreigner concerned more with himself than his "peeps."

David Maraniss
Pulitzer Prize–Winning Author of the 1999 Vince Lombardi Biography
When Pride Still Mattered

It has been generations since we worried about the Lions, and the Bears are always there as a historic rival. But Packers fans truly hate the Vikings. I really don't know what they'll do with all those tens of thousands of No. 4 jerseys they own. Probably put them in storage and take them out in seven years or so when he's going into Canton....

> "He is...a cheese-hating, beer-gagging, bratwurst-regurgitating foreigner concerned more with himself than his 'peeps.'"
> —Jeff Pearlman

I don't know if they'll boo Favre at Lambeau. I think it'll be more cheering louder for the Packers. I think what they'll really want is him to lose the two games against the Packers and throw six interceptions in those games. That would make them the happiest.... They'll forgive, but it'll take a while. In time they forgave Lombardi for going to Washington [to coach the Redskins]. This year, they'll hate [Favre] and hope he loses. But they'll forgive him when he goes into the Hall of Fame as a Packer. He has to go into Canton as a Packer, and that'll help.... It's really not even about Packers fans. They're jilted lovers. But it has nothing to do with them. It has to do with Ted Thompson first and foremost, and then Favre's age. He didn't want to quit playing, and the Packers were ready to move on without him. Favre's not really spurning Packers fans, but that's often not what the fan realizes.

THREE

Fans Love to Hate Brett Favre

Frank Cifaldi

Die-Hard Packers Fan and Favre Conspiracy Theorist

I used to love Brett Favre, I really did. I own a restaurant, Sammy's Pizza, in Cumberland, Wisconsin, and inside we had a shrine to Brett. There were pictures of him all over, including a few of him with my daughter. I own five Favre signed jerseys, a signed helmet, several signed balls—you name it, I got it. As odd as it sounds, my family even took a family vacation down to Mississippi one time to learn more about him. We went to his house and met with his brothers, we took pictures, and we ate at the Favre family restaurant. We also had a big fundraiser at the restaurant for his hometown after Hurricane Katrina. It was borderline passion/obsession, I think, but I just loved the guy. Well, that has obviously all changed.

Once he started talking about going to the Vikings, *everything* came down overnight. That was it. And I didn't just put that stuff in storage, either—I got rid of it. It was tainted. I did keep one jersey, though, but I had his name removed and a new one put on that reads "Benedict Arnold" to acknowledge just what a traitor the spoiled little brat really is. In some ways it felt like a messy divorce, I just felt so betrayed. It was very emotional for us, it really was. Hey, we cried when his dad died; we felt awful when we found out Deanna had cancer; we grieved for his family after the hurricane; and we all wept right alongside him at his tearful retirement speech. It was like we went through all of that right there with him. He was like a family member in some regards, it's crazy.

There have been so many little things. For instance, one time I sent him a letter apologizing for the fans' behavior after he had thrown for 24 interceptions in '93, and he sent me a really nice handwritten note, thanking me. Another time a picture of Brett holding my daughter, Emma, appeared on the cover of the *Green Bay Press Gazette* in conjunction with the celebration of his 200th consecutive start. So many memories all down the drain.

To be honest, I was okay when he went to the Jets. It was sad, but it was more of a case of the team going with the younger quarterback and preparing for the future. It hurt, but I could deal with it. When he did all of this stuff behind the scenes, though, to get with the Vikings, that was when I lost all respect for Brett Favre. For him to go to our archrival, it is beyond hurtful. He used to talk openly about how much he hated the Vikings and about how much he wanted to beat them, and now he is in bed with them. I don't get it. What a liar. It kills me, it really does. I am getting sweaty just talking about it. To see him wear purple is like a dagger through my heart.

I live in western Wisconsin in a lake community, and there are a lot of Minnesotans who have cabins up here. So we get a lot of Vikings fans that come into our restaurant. We have a lot of fun bantering back and forth, but this rivalry between Minnesota and Wisconsin is passionate. Our fans don't like each other. The first time I saw a guy come in wearing a purple Favre jersey I just about lost it. I immediately went over and told the guy that I liked his John David Booty jersey. It was pretty funny. Hell, the Vikings fans who know what a die-hard I am are wearing them in nonstop just to razz me. It's awful. I just don't understand how Vikings fans who hated Favre can now love him. I don't get it. But I am okay with it now, I am done with the guy. Minnesota, you can have him.

As for why he went to Minnesota? My theory on the whole thing goes back to when Ted Thompson didn't sign Randy Moss. I think Favre was done with the Packers right then and there. He was mad at Ted for not getting him the weapon he felt he needed and had apparently just had enough. In fact, he retired the *very* same day that Moss signed [a new contract] with the Patriots: March 3, 2008. He called up Mike McCarthy and said, "I'm done." That's a fact, you can look it up. Moss went there for a paltry fourth-round draft pick, too.

> "So many memories all down the drain....To see him wear purple is like a dagger through my heart."
> —Frank Cifaldi

Incidentally, we got Allen Barbre, an obscure right tackle, with our fourth pick that year. Look, I hated Randy Moss back then about as much as Vikings fans hated Brett Favre, but I was okay with him coming here because Brett really wanted him.

Anyway, about a month later, on April 4, an article came out in the *L.A. Times* by Sam Farmer that said Bus Cook [Favre's agent] was quietly shopping Favre around to other teams. Ted Thompson got hold of Favre, and they then talked about him returning to the Packers. Brett later decided that after talking it over with his wife that he wanted to stay retired, which I contend was all about him getting his unconditional release from the team. So the team went ahead and moved on with Rodgers, installing a new offense for him at the team's mini-camp, which ended on June 19. The next day Favre apparently called up and said he wanted to return to the team. That was when Thompson told him he was welcome to come back, but that he would have to compete for his old job.

I contend that Favre knew that the offense had been changed and knew it was "safe" and that the Packers would have moved on. That's why in April, after he had said he wanted to come back and the

As a New York Jet, Favre floundered in the second half of the 2008 season, failing to lead his team to the playoffs after an 8–3 start, prior to announcing his second retirement from football.

Packers were going to go to Mississippi, Favre called and said he had talked it over with Deanna and he was going to stay retired. Those phone calls to Minnesota weren't an enigma, the deal was already in place for him to go to Vikings. He wanted an outright release, and April was too soon, so he tried it again after the mini-camp. Had it all worked out, Brett would have then immediately gone to the Vikings in 2008 to get his revenge against Thompson. They didn't grant him his release, though, figuring something was up, and that was when they traded him to the Jets—as far away from Minnesota as possible.

Plus, they put in the poison pill in his contract, whereby if the Jets traded him back to Minnesota, it would cost them three first-round draft picks. I even called Farmer, at the *Times*, and he said that he stood by his story. He said "absolutely," but that he couldn't divulge his NFL source.

So that's my smoking-gun theory, and I'm sticking to it. Am I crazy? Maybe, but that's okay. Look, at the end of the day I wouldn't trade No. 12 for No. 4 right now, no way. We've got a guy with a lot of upside, and the Packer Nation feels good about that. I am sure Brett was pissed about Ted taking Aaron, too, but that was just a unique situation. I mean, when a guy who was projected by a lot of experts to be the No. 1 overall pick in the draft falls into your lap at No. 24, and you don't have to move up to get him, not to mention the fact that your guy has talked about retiring for the past two seasons, what are you going to do? You take Aaron Rodgers. Duh! What a no-brainer. You let him learn under a Hall of Fame quarterback and you let him hold a clipboard until Brett finally decides to retire. Well, guess what? Brett finally retired, so Ted went with Aaron. He wasn't forced out the door, no way. I am okay with that and so are most Packers fans. Ted is not the bad guy here, Brett is.

The only good that can possibly come of this is if Brett completely tanks and ruins the Vikings' season, that would be awesome. Otherwise, if he leads them back to the Super Bowl and gets them loss No. 5, that would be pretty good, too. Either way, we will be watching.

John O'Neill
Die-Hard Packers Fan Who Dresses as "Saint Vince" at Lambeau Field
This whole mess has really divided the Packer Nation in two. Some hate Brett, others hate Ted [Thompson], it is a big mess. I look at it like this: I appreciate what Brett did for this organization for the 16 years that he was here. But that was then and this is now. Now he is wearing purple, which makes him the sworn enemy. That is all there is to it. I don't wish him any ill will, or that he gets hurt or anything like that, but I have written him off. He is the enemy. And when he

comes to Green Bay, he will be treated as such. That is just the way it
is. I am not sure if I am going to boo him or not when he comes to
Lambeau, I just haven't made up my mind yet. It is going to be a surreal moment, that much is for sure. Some are already referring to it as
"Black Sunday." I have seen all sorts of creative ideas to celebrate the
day, too, including No. 4 shirts with the name "Judas." I had to buy
one of those, that was classic.

Yes, there is bad blood between Brett and Ted Thompson. That is
beyond being a theory, that is a fact—and both have diplomatically
said as much. As to why that relationship went south: theories abound
about it. The Randy Moss situation was certainly a part of it, but it is
much deeper than that. Ted used to be Enemy No. 1, but that has
passed. Sure, a lot of fans are still mad at him for the brutal way that
he let Brett go, but we are all happy with Aaron [Rodgers]. He is the
future of the franchise, and we have moved on.

This is way more than a rivalry, it's pure hatred. We don't like each
other. It is not so much the players who don't like each other, either, it
is the fans. We don't get along. There are a handful of fans in Wisconsin
who think that Chicago is our biggest rival, but I would say no way. I
think I can safely say that we collectively hate the Vikings a hell of a lot
more than the Bears. The rivalry used to be with Chicago, but in the
past 20 years it is all about beating Minnesota. You know, whenever
fans ask me for signed photos, I send them one with a caption that
reads "World Championships: Green Bay 12 and Minnesota 0. If God
didn't want it that way, it's safe to say that it wouldn't be that way." I
like to remind people that we have 12 World Championships up here,
but only three of them are Super Bowls.

Had he chosen to just stay retired, there is no doubt in my mind
that he would have remained *the* most popular person in Wisconsin
for years and years to come. Now, however, he is playing for the
enemy. A lot of people, I mean a lot, are really hurt by that. Twenty
years from now there will be fans who will have never forgiven him.
They are upset. As for me, I don't hate Brett. I am pretty mad at him,
but he gave us a lot of good years here. I thought about taking down

my Favre memorabilia, but it is still hanging up at this point. I will have to wait to see how he does against us this season, I think, before I start ripping stuff off the walls. But that is just me, I know of other fans who have gotten rid of it all. His legacy is tarnished, absolutely. It will forever be tainted. It's like if Bart Starr went and played for the Dallas Cowboys right after the Ice Bowl, only 100 times worse. That is how I feel about it.

Hey, the Vikings can have 11 Brett Favres on the field, for all I care. That team is cursed. They have been cursed since 1960, as far as I am concerned. They have been in the league for nearly 50 years and have nothing but cobwebs in their trophy cases. So one Brett Favre isn't going to change anything for those losers. He is basically being referred to now as part of the Cash for Clunkers program, so good luck, Minnesota! Purple is the color people turn when

> *"[The Vikings] have been in the league for nearly 50 years and have nothing but cobwebs in their trophy cases. So one Brett Favre isn' t going to change anything for those losers."*
> *—John O' Neill*

they choke, and who chokes more than the Vikings? Nobody. They invented the term. Look, I am just trying to focus on the positives. For starters, we all know how terrible Brett plays in domes. So let's hope he plays up there for a long, long time.

Tom Wiebe
Lifelong Packers Fan
Brett Favre was like a hero to me, an absolute legend. I was so inspired by the guy, I just loved his perseverance. But in the end he just gave up. He wanted to be the superstar and he screwed us over. So I am done with him. I mean, for him to choose to go to the Vikings, our most hated rival, that is such a slap in the face. If you are a true Green Bay fan, you understand. He wasn't the person we assumed he was. He didn't respect us at all. It was all about Brett. When you are a team

player and you make a career out of being the ultimate team guy, the guy you want to go to battle with, then how is this even possible? I sure as hell don't want to go to battle with Brett Favre anymore. No way. He wants to be the guy who will do whatever it takes to survive. He wants to be the guy with all the medals, and so what if everybody else dies.

Brett's all about Brett…and about greed, too. I mean, he got into an argument with his boss, but in the process of getting even with him he screws over thousands and thousands of Packers fans who were so loyal to the guy. It is unbelievable. Hey, Brett could have come back. They would have taken him back in a heartbeat. He could have come in and played alongside Aaron [Rodgers], but his ego wouldn't let him do it. That's the hubris of being Brett Favre. In the end I am a Packers fan, not a Brett Favre fan. I am done with him and I am done with his bullshit.

What rubs the fans the wrong way up here is that he sold us a bill of goods of who he was. His true character came out in this whole flip-flop saga. His ego has overcome the player that he was when he was with us. He was a different person when he was with us. He has changed. It's the hubris. His career is waning, he doesn't want to get out of the limelight; and he has become an absolute joke. His legacy is trashed as far as I am concerned. Will I boo him when he comes back to

> "I am a Packers fan, not a Brett Favre fan. I am done with him and…his bullshit."
> —Tom Wiebe

Lambeau wearing purple? No. That is not my style. I will sit in silence. If the entire stadium sat silent, that would send a stronger message to him in my opinion. Does he deserve to be in the Packers' Hall of Fame? Yes, he deserves it for what he did while he was here. But he will never be revered here the way Bart [Starr] or Ray [Nitschke] or Vince [Lombardi] were. Never. Not anymore. Brett is not like Reggie White, who always had a higher cause. Brett is just out for himself. Good riddance. Minnesota, you can have him.

Craig Schroepfer
Longtime Packers Fan

To see him wear purple is pretty surreal, to be honest. It is a sight I truly never thought I would see in my lifetime, that is for sure. It is like that moment in pro wrestling where your hero turns into a villain— that is how Green Bay fans feel about Favre now. He turned on us. I have two buddies who are going to get rid of all their Favre memorabilia because they are so pissed off at what he did. It is emotional for a lot of people, it really is. You basically have two sides in Wisconsin: those who now hate Brett and those loyalists who still love him, but hate Ted Thompson instead. They blame him and him alone for this mess. A lot of it goes back to the Randy Moss stuff, where we could have had him for a fourth-round draft pick. Favre was obviously pissed that he didn't go out and get him, and I think that was the beginning of the end. The media just ran with it from there. You know, the media just loves the guy, and I am not quite sure why. He has a messiah complex and just loves the attention. The running joke when he went to New York to play with the Jets in 2008 was, "Good for Brett, he will finally get the attention he feels he deserves." In the end, it is just a crazy story, and people, for whatever their reasons, just can't seem to get enough of it. I will just close with this last thought: in my mind, no matter what Brett Favre does from here on out, he will always be a Jet.

Joel Staats
Former University of Minnesota Football Player and Wisconsin Native

It's tough to see old No. 4 wearing purple, that is for sure. I am a die-hard Pack fan and seeing this happen has been rough. I will say this, though: I am a Green Bay Packers fan way before I am a Brett Favre fan. I still admire him as a quarterback, but I definitely think he has tarnished his legacy as one of the NFL's all-time greats by choosing to play with the rival Vikings. I cheered for the guy for 16 years and cried along with him at his retirement ceremony. So I feel like this is a big stab in the back, to be honest. On a side note, I have enjoyed watching the Minnesota fans having to put up with his retirement shenanigans over the past year—something us Packers fans knew all too well during the latter stages of his time in Green Bay. We didn't care at the time, though, because we always figured he would retire as a Packer in the end. So we are upset and rightfully so. I will say this, though: living in the Twin Cities and seeing it from the other side is definitely a crazy perspective.

Bill Wenzel
President of Titletown Tickets
From a business standpoint, Brett Favre was great for our business over the years. No question. I mean, his hinting about retiring for about four years only helped us sell more tickets. Fans wanted to see him play in what could be his last game and were willing to pay big bucks for that. So that was fabulous. Brett was a personality that people came to see. He was larger than life in some regards.

From a personal standpoint, I don't have a problem with Brett playing in Minnesota. The reality is that the Packers made a business decision. Brett retired and then wanted to come back, and ultimately the team decided to move on. Anybody that has ever run a business knows that you can't have employees treating the company like that. If they did, you wouldn't be in business very long. You have to have a long-term view of success for your company, as well, and in this situation the organization decided to move on with Aaron Rodgers. He was the best quarterback on the roster at that time, and they acted accordingly. Had they not, they probably would have lost Aaron that next year as a free agent. So they had to make a decision. I am sure it was a tough call, but in the end I think they are better off for having done so. Aaron is the future of this franchise now, and we have all moved on.

The bottom line is this: Brett made it personal. Ted Thompson and the Packers organization never made it personal, they have been nothing but first-class throughout this entire saga. Brett is the one who wants to get revenge and stick it to Ted. That is the No. 1 thing that has turned off Packers fans to Brett Favre. It isn't so much that he still wants to play—heck, he can play until he is 50 for all I care—it is the fact that he wants to play for the Vikings just so he can get even, in his eyes.

You know, when Brett left in 2008 the anger was directed squarely at Ted because he "let Brett go." But now in 2009 the sentiment is heavily in favor of Ted and very negative toward Brett. What Brett did by signing with Minnesota was to prove that Ted was 100 percent right last year in trading him away to the Jets. He unknowingly vindicated him. And not only did Brett screw over the Packers, he also screwed over the Jets. He convinced them that he was going to retire, so they released him. He lied to them. They could have traded him and gotten value. Instead, they moved way up in the draft to get [Mark] Sanchez, which was a big leap of faith for them. I feel badly for the Jets, I really do. They got screwed.

When Brett runs out onto Lambeau Field on November 1, he is going to be resoundingly booed. There will be a smattering of cheers, but for the most part he is going to get what the fans here think he deserves. It is a state divided right now, though, that is for sure. He will eventually be in the Ring of Honor, though, because time heals all wounds. Look, in the end I think the Packers got sick and tired of Brett's games. He is still playing them, too—look what happened in Minnesota. The Vikings were held hostage and ultimately caved into every one of his demands. I had to laugh when I saw he signed a two-year contract. I hope you love drama, Vikings fans, because all of the retirement talk that we had to put up with over the years is now coming your way after the season. We've been there, done that. Trust me, it's no fun.

Sue Thurston
Wife of Packers Great Fuzzy Thurston and Co-Owner of Titletown Tickets and Fuzzy's 63 Bar and Grill in Green Bay

To say I am disappointed would be such an understatement. Brett *was* my favorite Packer. Not anymore. My husband, Fuzzy, and I have known Brett for a long, long time. He even wrote the foreword for

Fuzzy's biography years ago. He was like family to so many of us. So we are really beside ourselves about this whole thing. I mean, why go to Minnesota of all places? The Vikings? Oh, that stings. I cannot and will not root for him as a Viking. I could live with him finishing his career with the Jets, but not the Vikings. He brought me a lot of joy in my life, and I can't forget that, but what he did by going to our bitter rival was very disrespectful. So why not go somewhere else? It's not like he needs the money anymore. It's just beyond disappointing. It is so hurtful, just a real slap across the face of the fans who supported him for all those years. If it's to get revenge against Ted Thompson, that is so petty because we, the fans, are the ones being punished for it. It's not fair.

I am only remembering Brett in my memories. Some of the fans just can't let go. I read about one family in the paper whose whole basement was green and gold and now they are repainting it all purple. It's just crazy. In fact, once he signed with Minnesota, I took down all my pictures of him. I didn't throw them away, although I thought about it. They are in storage for now. I have one in particular that he signed for me that reads, "To Sue, from your favorite Packer...too bad, Fuzzy!" That one was especially hard to take down because it meant an awful lot to me. We are leaving all of his things up at the restaurant, but at home it all had to come down. I am hoping that time heals all wounds, but we will have to wait and see. I will always love Brett, but it's going to take a while for me to even think about forgiving him.

> "It's just beyond disappointing. It is so hurtful, just a real slap across the face of the fans who supported him for all those years."
> —Sue Thurston

The game in Green Bay on November 1 is going to be unlike anything we have ever seen before. The thought of Brett running out of that tunnel wearing a purple uniform is just sickening. I don't know what I am going to do—it is going to be pretty odd to say the least.

A Packers fan supports new starting quarterback Aaron Rodgers (No. 12) while taking a slap at Favre (No. 4) at a 2008 victory over the Indianapolis Colts at Lambeau Field. *Photo courtesy of Getty Images*

You see, Brett was truly beloved in Green Bay. When his dad died, it was like a family member had passed. We mourned right along with him. People are naturally pretty upset. It's like he deserted us after all we had been through together. I guess the best-case scenario for us, as Green Bay fans, is for Brett to lead the Vikings back to the Super Bowl, only so that they can lose No. 5. That would make me happy— No. 4 leading Minnesota to No. 5. Go Packers!

"Mr. Yoder II"

Blogger

By now, everyone should know how I personally feel about Brett Favre. He is the most self-absorbed, selfish star athlete of our time. No player in the last 25 years, save a few brain-damaged boxers, has so tarnished their own legacy. To string along an entire franchise in the Minnesota Vikings and their two potential starting quarterbacks [Sage Rosenfels and Tarvaris Jackson] has been disgraceful. No player, not even Brett the Great, is entitled to skipping training camp that every other player in the league has to attend. In his own mind, Favre must imagine himself riding into Minnesota on a white horse, the savior of a franchise. However, the rest of us see him for what he truly is, a washed-up ex-quarterback, arriving into town atop a jackass, how appropriate.

> "He is the most self-absorbed, selfish star athlete of our time. No player in the last 25 years, save a few brain-damaged boxers, has so tarnished their own legacy."
> — "Mr. Yoder II"

Adam Warwas

Blogger

Perhaps nobody hates Brett Favre more than Sage Rosenfels does right now. I am a close second. I'll admit it. I tell everyone. I tell the readers of [my] site. I tell my coworkers. I tell my wife. I tell my friends. I tell the guy at the urinal next to me. And you can bet your ass I'd tell Brett Favre if I had the chance. The guy has ruined Vikings football year-in and year-out. He is the definition of the word "nemesis." He's a wishy-washy, over-hyped, media-milking, interception-chucking, tear-duct using, microphone-sucking, money-grubbing, tractor-riding, and wrangler-wearing *Packer*! The last word of that run-on sentence is meant to be the most insulting. He will always be a Packer, regardless of what color he wears this year. Not only is he *a* Packer, he's *the* Packer. It would be the equivalent of Adrian Peterson becoming a

Packer. This whole thing is pissing on the very traditions that make Vikings football as great as we all like to think it is.

Brian Nordling
Die-Hard Vikings Fan

I am a die-hard Vikings fan, and I have never liked Favre. Ever. This whole thing is nuts. If we were going to go out and get a washed-up quarterback, then maybe we should have looked at John Elway. Look, I think we are better with him than without him, but he is the enemy. He always has been. To see him in purple is too weird. Hell, my kid came home from his friend's house the other day wearing a purple Favre jersey, and my wife and I just about hit the floor. We have a lot of Packers fans in our neighborhood, and one of them put him up to it, obviously. They all thought that was pretty funny. Yeah, ha, ha. Seeing that on my own flesh and blood was almost too much to take. We are sort of doomed either way, as far as I see it. I mean, if we do terribly this year and he throws a ton of interceptions, the Packers fans are going to be thrilled. But if we go ahead and run the table and win the Super Bowl, then we are going to have to listen to the cheeseheads needle us to death about how it was "their guy" who finally got us our first championship. So either way, we are kind of screwed. The whole thing has caused me a lot of anxiety to be quite honest. That is the problem we have here in Minnesota, there are way too many Packers fans who live here. Way too many.

> *"Brett Favre screwed the Green Bay Packers fans! Let that soak in awhile..."*
> — *Michael McDonald*

They are everywhere. I mean, we aren't all moving to Wisconsin, so what is up with this? I shouldn't have to worry about my kid being brainwashed every time he walks down the street, for God's sake. It is too crazy. The bottom line is this: I am going to root for the Vikings no matter who is playing quarterback. And I hope to hell he destroys the Packers in both games this season, especially in Green Bay. But, and this is big, there is no way I would ever draft Favre in my fantasy-football league. That is where I have to draw the line.

Zac Wassink
Blogger
Brett Favre has completed his "heel-turn." When I was growing up, Hulk Hogan was the quintessential good guy in the WWF. Hogan taught us kids to say our prayers and take our vitamins. He never took shortcuts in order to win. He saved the damsel in distress and carried the American flag. Hogan continued this persona once he joined WCW in 1994. That is, until 1996, when Hogan joined with "The Outsiders" to create the New World Order. After turning heel, Hogan traded in his red and yellow attire for black pants and black boots. He sported a dark beard, strummed Jimi Hendrix tunes on the spray-painted WCW belt, and became the ultimate bad guy. Ladies and gentlemen, I present Brett Favre.... When Hollywood Hogan returned to the [now] WWE several years ago, he was cheered by the fans as a "face," a good guy, because the fans respected and adored him. Brett Favre may get cheers in the dome when he throws a touchdown for the Vikings. The rest of us, though, will now remember Favre as the guy who dropped the leg on the entire state of Wisconsin.

Michael McDonald
Blogger
Even though Favre was known as "Mr. Packer," he rarely made concessions to his salary to help the Packers with their cap space. Maybe some more talent could have been brought in, and they could have won more than one championship during his tenure. It comes down to this. All of Brett Favre's actions and drama affected the coaches, teammates, and the GM. He also affected the team's success and bottom line. That affects the owners of the Green Bay Packers. The Packers are publicly owned. That means that ultimately Brett Favre *screwed* the Green Bay Packers *fans!* Let that soak in awhile...

SOURCES

Introduction: Why I Love to Hate Brett Favre

"I WAS 18 AND DEANNA WAS 19 WHEN SHE GOT PREGNANT...": "Brett Favre Timeline," by Jimmy Traina, *Sports Illustrated*, September 5, 2002.

Players Hate Brett Favre

PAUL HORNUNG: "Paul Hornung to Brett Favre: Stick Around," by Fred Mitchell. *Chicago Tribune*. May 13, 2009.

MARK CHMURA: First six quotes: "Mark Chmura: Favre Signed Now 'Cause He Didn't Want to Go to Camp," 540-AM ESPN Milwaukee. August 19, 2009. Last four quotes: *The Homer Show*, 540-AM ESPN Milwaukee. August 18, 2009.

GILBERT BROWN: *The Homer Show*, 540-AM ESPN Milwaukee. August 18, 2009.

DON BEEBE: *The Homer Show*, 540-AM ESPN Milwaukee. August 20, 2009.

TRENT DILFER: *The Homer Show*, 540-AM ESPN Milwaukee. August 21, 2009.

CRIS CARTER: *The Homer Show*, 540-AM ESPN Milwaukee. August 19, 2009.

RODNEY HARRISON: "Harrison Rips Vikes for Signing Favre," by Mark Craig. *Star Tribune*. September 3, 2009.

NICK BARNETT: "Favre Comes Back 'For the Right Reasons,'" by Jason Wilde, *Wisconsin State Journal*. August 19, 2009.

AL HARRIS: "Favre Comes Back 'For the Right Reasons,'" by Jason Wilde, *Wisconsin State Journal*. August 19, 2009.

AARON RODGERS: Michael Irvin's ESPN Radio Show, ESPN.com. 2008.

TROY BROWN: "Vikings Players Won't Question Brad Childress' Flip-Flop on Brett Favre—As Long as They Win," by Sean Jensen, *Pioneer Press,* September 8, 2009.

MARK SCHLERETH: "Ex-NFL Players Rip Minnesota Vikings QB Brett Favre, Coach Brad Childress," by Sean Jensen, *Pioneer Press.* August 21, 2009.

The Media Hate Brett Favre

GENE WOJCIECHOWSKI: "Favre's Left Green Bay Behind, for Good," by Gene Wojciechowski, ESPN.com. August 18, 2009.

MIKE FLORIO: "Favre, Vikings Likely Had Deal Two Months Ago," by Mike Florio, *Sporting News.* August 19, 2009.

JEFF PEARLMAN: "We Love Comebacks, but Favre's Return Will Tarnish His Legacy," by Jeff Pearlman, *Sports Illustrated.* August 18, 2009.

DAVID MARANISS: "Favre's a Viking, but Is He a Villain?" by Don Banks. SI.com, August 19, 2009.

Fans Hate Brett Favre

MR. YODER II: "Brett Favre in His Own Words," by Mr. Yoder II, www.randallsimonssausages.com. August 19, 2009.

ADAM WARWAS: "Handbook: For Those Who Love the Vikings but Hate Brett Favre," by Adam Warwas, VikingsGab.com. August 20, 2009.

ZAC WASSINK: "Brett Favre Has Become Hollywood Hulk Hogan," by Zac Wassink, Associated Content, Inc. August 18, 2009.

MICHAEL MCDONALD: "The Top 10 Reasons I Hate Brett Favre," by Michael McDonald, BleacherReport.com.

Brett Favre gets slapped on the head by Minnesota Vikings defensive end Kenny Mixon after throwing a pass in a game at the Metrodome on November 17, 2002. Mixon got flagged for a 15-yard personal foul.

The Giants' Corey Webster (above) intercepts a Favre pass intended for Donald Driver during overtime of the NFC Championship Game on January 20, 2008, setting up New York's game-winning field goal. The NFL career leader in interceptions, Favre (right) reacts after throwing a pick against the Jacksonville Jaguars in 2004.

Often described as "just a big kid who loves to play the game," Brett Favre is perhaps the most polarizing quarterback in the NFL. While his stats are undeniable, and Favre is destined for the Pro Football Hall of Fame one day, his playful attitude grates on some. Others dislike his indecisiveness over the last several years. People either love him or hate him...or both.

While quarterbacking the New York Jets, Brett Favre (left) rips off his chin strap after throwing an interception during the fourth quarter of a 24–17 loss to the Miami Dolphins on December 28, 2008, at Giants Stadium. Having played poorly in the second half of the season and missing the playoffs, Favre retired for the second year in a row. By August, after changing his mind yet again, he signed with his old archrival, the Minnesota Vikings, to be their quarterback for the 2009 season.

Favre (left) drops back to pass against Kansas City in the Metrodome on August 21, 2009, in a preseason 17–13 victory over the Chiefs. A Vikings fan (above) expresses her love for Brett Favre at Ford Field in Week 2 of the regular season, before a 27–13 win over the Lions. *Photos courtesy of Getty Images*

No. 4 Brett Favre dons the Vikings horned helmet during training camp on August 18, 2009, in Eden Prairie, Minnesota, the day he flew up from Mississippi to sign with the team.

I LOVE BRETT FAVRE

The **Brett Favre** Fans Love to **Love**

ROSS BERNSTEIN

TRIUMPH
BOOKS

Copyright © 2009 by Ross Bernstein

No part of this publication may be reproduced, stored in a retrieval system, or transmitted, in any form by any means, electronic, mechanical, photocopying, or otherwise, without the prior written permission of the publisher, Triumph Books, 542 S. Dearborn St., Suite 750, Chicago, Illinois 60605.

Triumph Books and colophon are registered trademarks of Random House, Inc.

This book is available in quantity at special discounts for your group or organization. For further information, contact:

Triumph Books
542 South Dearborn Street
Suite 750
Chicago, Illinois 60605
(312) 939-3330
Fax (312) 663-3557
www.triumphbooks.com

Printed in U.S.A.
ISBN: 978-1-60078-376-0

Design and editorial production by Prologue Publishing Services, LLC
Photos courtesy of AP Images except where otherwise indicated

CONTENTS

Why I Love Brett Favre

WHEN I FIRST HEARD THAT BRETT FAVRE was going to play for the Vikings, I figured it was just another vile Internet rumor. Come on, are you kidding me? No. 4, playing for the purple? Yeah…right. And it wasn't just that he was going to *play* for the Vikings, it was that he actually *wanted* to play for the Vikings. There's a big difference. Let me get this straight. Arguably the greatest Packer in history wants to play for his team's biggest rival, the Vikings? I was skeptical, but when the rumors wouldn't go away, I started to wonder if this was all some sort of cruel and blasphemous hoax. Look, I have written more than 40 sports books in my day and have been able to chronicle more than my fair share of fascinating stories over the years, but I have to be honest, nothing has ever rocked my world like the thought of Brett Favre *wanting* to wear purple.

It's no secret that we Minnesotans don't care too much for the Packers. It goes both ways, too, they despise us just as much if not more. It's been that way for nearly 50 years. What we have up here in the great north woods is the quintessential border battle: two states, separated by Lake Superior to the north and the St. Croix River to the south, that don't particularly care for one another—at least not when

it comes to sports. And it's not just the Vikings and Packers, the Gophers and Badgers don't get along, either. In fact, the University of Minnesota and the University of Wisconsin have the longest Division I rivalry in college football history, going all the way back to 1890. Trust me, I know about the intensity of it firsthand. You see, after a failed attempt to make it as a walk-on with Minnesota's hockey team back in the late '80s, I wound up becoming the school mascot, "Goldy the Gopher." Safe to say, I had my fair share of run-ins over the years with my arch-nemesis, "Bucky the Badger." In my eyes, however, rodents will always be above weasels in the food chain, but I digress.

> For the better part of the past two decades, Favre has been Enemy No. 1 in Minnesota. I mean, this guy has just killed us over the years. His fourth-quarter comebacks have become the stuff of legend.

When it comes to football in Minnesota, the Vikings reign supreme. We live and die with this team, no question. I grew up worshipping the vaunted Purple People Eaters—Alan Page, Jim Marshall, and Carl Eller; along with Chuck Foreman, Ahmad Rashad, and of course quarterback Fran Tarkenton. I idolized that guy. I mean, in my backyard, I *was* "Fran the Man." I am not sure if I ever took off his No. 10 jersey long enough for Mom to actually wash it. I wore that ratty thing so much it actually turned from purple to brown. I was programmed from a very early age in my household to despise the Packers. They were the enemy.

I remember going to my first game at Lambeau Field. I was in college and road-tripped over with about 50 fraternity brothers. Don "the Magic Man" Majkowski was calling the plays in those days, and as such, getting tickets was no problem. I have to admit, being in Lambeau was a pretty neat experience. To be honest, I was really jealous. After watching games in that awful Metrodome for so many years, I had now finally seen the light for how football *should* be

played—outside with a lot of liquor and smoked, cured meats. What a place, so much history and so many die-hard fans. It was, like, 15 degrees and there were people out tailgating and having a ball. I have vague memories of tailgating at old Metropolitan Stadium as a kid, but nothing like this. These folks had this stuff down to a science; I was impressed. I had never seen so many grills fired up at one time, not to mention the sheer volume of beer that was being consumed. I think the cumulative blood-alcohol level come game time was about 6.1. And it was a noon kickoff!

Well, once Brett Favre hit the town in the early '90s, everything changed. Needless to say, no longer could you purchase a block of 50 tickets for a home game in Green Bay. Favre completely reenergized that fan base and turned the whole organization around. It was nothing short of remarkable. Sadly, however, their success over the ensuing years would oftentimes come at Minnesota's expense. Safe to say that for the better part of the past two decades, Favre has been Enemy No. 1 in Minnesota. I mean, this guy has just killed us over the years. His fourth-quarter comebacks have become the stuff of legend. I have had more than my share of purple hangovers during that time and way *too many* of them have been courtesy of *that* guy. Perhaps the most painful one came back in 2000 on *Monday Night Football*, when he threw a bomb to Antonio Freeman that was deflected by cornerback Chris Dishman, only to see Freeman somehow bobble the ball, catch it on his back, get up, and then run it in for the game-winning touchdown. I was beyond pissed after that one, and that was just one of *many*.

So, when I heard about Favre wanting to come here back in 2008, after he had retired and then unretired and then retired again from the Packers, I was suspicious as to what his ulterior motive was. Was this all some sort of clever ruse? Was he plotting some sort of Trojan-horse ambush upon us by coming here and then sabotaging our team? As I dug deeper, I found out that the rumors were indeed real. Turned out there was a backstory to this improbable saga, a genesis to what ultimately led me, and so many others like me, to go from *hating Brett Favre to loving Brett Favre*.

The Backstory...

The rumors surrounding Favre's first retirement began back in 2003. He was in his mid-thirties, and many felt like he had just burned out— physically as well as emotionally. He had played for 11 seasons in the league up until then, led the team to a Super Bowl victory, set all sorts of records, and had even signed a 10–year contract extension worth around $100 million back in 2001. Needless to say, there probably wasn't much left to prove at that point. Favre loved to play the game, though, and he loved to win, so he kept coming back for what would turn out to be a whole bunch of just-one-more-seasons.

Long known for his toughness and superhuman ability to play through pain, Favre had never missed a start in his career. That all nearly came to an end on December 22, 2003, however, when he suited up to play in a *Monday Night Football* game against Oakland. What made the game so significant was the fact that his father, Irv, had just died of a heart attack one day earlier. Everybody knew how close he was to his dad, his best friend and former high school football coach, and nobody expected him to play that night. Favre felt other-wise, though, and decided to go for it, figuring that was what "Big Irv" would have wanted him to do. That night, millions of sports fans tuned in to watch what would go down as one of the gutsiest per-formances in NFL history. With a heavy heart and an occasional tear, Favre went out and threw for four touchdowns on nearly 400 yards passing in a 41–7 rout of the Raiders. In many people's eyes, that was the night the legend of Brett Favre was born.

From there, Favre went through more than his fair share of ups and downs—both on and off the field. Just 10 months after his father's death, his brother-in-law was killed in an all-terrain-vehicle accident on Favre's Mississippi property. Soon after in 2004, Favre's wife, Deanna, was diagnosed with breast cancer. Then, in August 2005, Favre's family was rocked by Hurricane Katrina when it blew through Mississippi, destroying his family's home in Kiln and exten-sively damaging his own property in Hattiesburg. Despite all of this, though, Favre continued to play on.

On December 22, 2003—one day after the death of his father, Irv—Brett Favre threw for 399 yards and four TDs against the Oakland Raiders on *Monday Night Football*, cementing his legend.

Photo courtesy of Getty Images

In 2005 Ted Thompson took over as the team's general manager and wound up drafting Cal quarterback Aaron Rodgers with their first-round pick. Projected by many to be one of the first players chosen, Rodgers fell to the Packers at No. 24. Favre, who was hoping that the team would use that pick on a stud wide receiver or mammoth offensive lineman who would help him rebuild the offense, instead now had to deal with the fact that the organization had just named his heir apparent. After finishing the season with a dismal 4–12 record, Mike Sherman was let go as the team's head coach. Favre lobbied for his friend, former Packers assistant coach Steve Mariucci, to get an interview for the head-coaching position, but for whatever reason he was not one of the eight finalists for the job. This is where the relationship between Favre and Ted Thompson started to go south.

Speculation that Favre was going to hang 'em up soon started to catch fire. In an interview with ESPN shortly after the season, Favre said, "If I had to pick right now and make a decision, I'd say I'm not coming back." With little to no communication between Favre and the Packers that off-season about whether or not he was going to return, Favre touched a nerve on September 3, 2006, while speaking with Bob Costas on HBO's *Costas Now* program: "If it comes to a point where they do start over and I feel like I can play, and they say, 'Brett, if you want to go somewhere else, go ahead, we've got to start over. It's time for us to rebuild.' If I've got the itch at some point, I can't say no." For many Packers fans, the writing was on the wall.

Favre came back and led the team to an 8–8 record that next season. Following the team's 26–7 season-ending win over the Bears, Favre finally addressed the big elephant in the room during his postgame interview with NBC's Andrea Kremer: "If today's my last game, I want to remember it. It's tough. It's tough. I'll miss these guys, I'll miss this game." Then, after a month of deliberation, and to the relief of Packers fans everywhere, Favre announced that he was "excited about coming back" for yet another season. That March a reinvigorated Favre pushed hard for Ted Thompson to acquire electrifying wide receiver Randy Moss, who wanted out of Oakland.

Moss, who had torched the Packers on numerous occasions while playing with the Vikings, would be the "missing piece" to the puzzle in Favre's eyes. He apparently pleaded with Thompson to make a deal to get him, but to no avail. That April Moss wound up being traded to New England for the mere pittance of a fourth-round draft pick. Favre was not pleased.

Upset, Favre pressed on and led the team all the way to the NFC Championship Game that season before ultimately losing to the Giants at Lambeau Field in overtime following a crucial interception deep in Packers territory. Immediately following the game, neither Favre nor coach Mike McCarthy would comment on whether or not Favre would be returning for the 2008 season. Sure enough, on

> *"If today's my last game, I want to remember it. It's tough. It's tough. I'll miss these guys, I'll miss this game."*
> —*Brett Favre (2006)*

March 6, 2008, Favre, after playing in 275 straight games, officially retired from the Packers. Ironically, it would come just days after the Patriots re-signed Randy Moss to a three-year, $27 million deal.

"I'd like to thank the Packers for giving me the opportunity," he said at his retirement press conference. "I hope that every penny that they've spent on me they know was money well-spent. It was never about the money or fame or records, and I hear people talk about your accomplishments and things.... It was never my accomplishments, it was our accomplishments, the teammates that I've played with, and I can name so many. It was never about me, it was about everybody else. It just so happens the position I played got most of the attention. But the Packers, it's been a great relationship, and I hope that this organization and the fans appreciate me as much as I appreciate them.... I've given everything I possibly can give to this organization, to the game of football, and I don't think I've got anything left to give, and that's it. I know I can play, but I don't think I want to. And that's really what it comes down to.... I will wonder if I made the wrong

decision. I'm sure on Sundays, I will say, 'I could be doing that, I should be doing that.' ... Will I find something to do that's equal to throwing a touchdown pass at Lambeau Field? I doubt it. I'm not even going to try. ... I'm no fool. I know there is nothing out there like that. But life does go on. I will do something. It will be nice for a while to not feel like I have to live up to certain expectations. I can just ride off into the sunset."

Then, just a few weeks later, Favre had second thoughts about retiring, and the Packers agreed to let him return to the team. But, according to reports in the *Milwaukee Journal Sentinel*, Favre got cold feet and backed out at the last minute, just as Mike McCarthy and Ted Thompson were about to fly to Mississippi to seal the deal. To the dismay of some and the affirmation of others, the Packers then, for all intents and purposes, committed to Aaron Rodgers as their starting quarterback. Several days later the *L.A. Times* reported that Favre's agent, Bus Cook, had been making inquiries to other teams about their interest in trading for the three-time MVP.

"That's the last thing I'm thinking about," Favre told *Sports Illustrated*. "I have no idea where that came from, but it certainly didn't come from me. I'm happy about my decision, and I haven't once said, 'I wonder if I made the wrong decision?' I know it's the right one. It's kind of funny. Even when I'm retired, they won't let me stay retired."

Further speculation ran rampant as fans pleaded with management to entice Favre back out of retirement. Thompson dug in his heels, however, and remained firmly committed to starting the season with Rodgers. Conspiracy theories started to run wild, and before long Packer Nation was a country divided—one side going with Favre and the other with Thompson. In April Favre added fuel to the fire when he told the *Biloxi Sun-Herald* that there was still a possibility of his returning to Green Bay if Rodgers got hurt and they asked him to come back.

"It would be hard to pass up, I guess," Favre, then 38, told Sam Farmer of the *L.A. Times* in April. "But three months from now, say

that presents itself, I may say, 'You know what, I'm so glad I made that decision. I feel very comfortable in what I'm doing and my decision.' Yeah, I can probably be up there doing that and playing, but again, I don't know. It's only speculation. I think the world of that team. I had a lot of fun, not only this year, but over my career. Those guys I played with this past year, a lot of young guys, a lot of fun.... If that opportunity presented itself and they did call, it would be tempting. And I very well could be enticed to do it."

> *"I have no idea where that came from, but it certainly didn't come from me. I'm happy about my decision, and I haven't once said, 'I wonder if I made the wrong decision?' I know it's the right one. It's kind of funny. Even when I'm retired, they won't let me stay retired."*
>
> *—Brett Favre (2008)*

Thompson went to Mississippi to visit Favre in May but didn't get the sense Favre was having serious thoughts about playing again. That June, according to an article in the *Milwaukee Journal Sentinel*, Favre contacted the team about coming out of retirement, only to get rebuffed. Favre later said that he was offered the opportunity to come back to the team, because he was still under contract at $12 million per year, to essentially compete for the starting quarterback job with Rodgers. Feeling disrespected, that July Favre sent the Packers a letter requesting his unconditional release from the team so that he could presumably play elsewhere, a move that caught everybody in Green Bay off guard. Rumors then started to swirl that Favre wanted to do the unthinkable, sign with the hated Minnesota Vikings—a move most chalked up to petty revenge. Just the thought of Favre wearing purple was an unconscionable slap across the collective face of Packers fans everywhere.

"I knew that at some point somebody else has to be the quarterback of this team," Favre would later tell ESPN Radio's Ed Werder.

"I knew how the game works. Look, if Joe Montana could get traded [from San Francisco to Kansas City], as great as he is, then it could happen to anyone. I never thought that could happen to me, but I am proof positive that it can.... I was a little peeved, I guess. It was like there was someone sitting on each shoulder, talking to me as I went back and forth. Part of me wanted to stick it to them, but then the other side was like, 'No, those are the wrong reasons.' My pride was hurt a little bit, I guess."

The Packers responded with a statement saying that they weren't planning on granting Favre's request for release and remained committed to Rodgers as their starter, even if Favre decided to return to the team. "We've communicated that to Brett, that we have since moved forward," Thompson said to the Associated Press. "At the same time, we've never said that there couldn't be some role that he might play here. But I would understand his point that he would want to play."

> Rumors then started to swirl that Favre wanted to do the unthinkable, sign with the hated Minnesota Vikings...an unconscionable slap across the collective face of Packers fans everywhere.

Shortly thereafter, in mid-July, Favre sat down with Fox News' Greta Van Susteren to tell his side of the story. At this point he wanted to not only set the record straight but also put pressure on the Packers to either release him outright or trade him, so that he could play that upcoming season with someone else. He told her:

> One of the things that people, from what I understand, are saying is that I retired because the Packers or Ted Thompson didn't ask me back. That's totally untrue. They wanted an answer before free agency and the draft. Mike McCarthy called every week. After about a two- or three-week grace period after the season, Mike would call: "Hey, how's things going, you know? Where are you at with your decision?"

"Boy, Mike, I'm kind of burned out right now and just need some time." I said, "Boy, it'd be nice if I could wait until training camp."

"Well, you know, we have a different direction we got to go in, you know? If you're not going to be here, we have to sign someone." Which is fine. I totally understand that. But I was not ready to totally commit. Regardless of what people think, the bottom line, March 3, when I got in front of the podium, did I want to play? Yes. One hundred percent? No. And I think people who have followed my career, people who know me closely, know that I won't play if I'm not 100 percent committed. I could have easily said, "You know what? I'll take the money, I'll come back, and hopefully, I'll get committed somewhere either before training camp, during training camp, or during the season. No one will know." But that's not me....

[As far as playing with another team] it's unfortunate that it has come to this. And I'm sure there are a lot of fans out there thinking, from what they've heard, that Brett is a traitor, he wants to play elsewhere. That's not true. I was told that playing in Green Bay was not an option, regardless what you hear from up there. You know, I'm not making it up. I was told that playing in Green Bay was not an option. And then I was told that, "We can't imagine you playing" or "[we] can't envision you playing with another team, as well." What does that tell me? It tells me, "We don't want you playing, period."...

I'm guilty of one thing and that's retiring early, I knew that I would have second thoughts. So, I mean, you're telling me playing there is not an option? "Playing elsewhere, we just can't, we're trying to protect your legacy." Well, thank you. I appreciate that. But, apparently, now they're wanting to protect my legacy by bringing me back and having me be a backup.

[As for playing for the Vikings] I've never envisioned that. I mean, I've heard all the talk, like everyone else. It's hard not to. But, you know, I mean, that's always been our biggest rival, obviously, [along] with the Bears. And did I ever think of that? No. Did I ever think it would happen? Absolutely not. And by getting a release, obviously, it gives you an option.

> "I was told that playing in Green Bay was not an option. And then I was told that, 'We...can't envision you playing with another team.' ... What does that tell me? It tells me, 'We don't want you playing, period.'"
> —Brett Favre (2008)

The next day the Packers filed tampering charges against the Vikings with the league office, alleging improper communication between Vikings offensive coordinator Darrell Bevell (Favre's good friend and former quarterbacks coach in Green Bay) as well as Vikings head coach Brad Childress—whom Favre had gotten to know over the years as an acquaintance. (The NFL maintains strict anti-tampering rules that ban teams from approaching players who are under contract elsewhere.) After an investigation, however, commissioner Roger Goodell ruled there had been no violation of tampering rules. Then, on July 29, Favre formally filed for reinstatement with the NFL, which was granted by Goodell, effective August 4. The newly unretired Favre then flew up to Green Bay to report to Packers training camp. Speculation was running wild as to whether or not they would sign him after all. It was an absolute media circus. After a lengthy meeting with Mike McCarthy and Ted Thompson, however, both sides agreed it was time to sever the umbilical cord. The Brett Favre era was officially over.

Or was it? Two days later team president Mark Murphy reportedly offered Favre a $25 million lifetime marketing agreement to represent the Packers in an official capacity and, more important, to

remain retired. Favre said no, thanks. Incidentally, the Packers had planned on retiring Favre's jersey in the *Monday Night Football* season opener at Lambeau Field. Their opponent that evening: Minnesota. Needless to say, that idea got scrapped—despite the fact that it had already been heavily advertised and promoted.

Fearing Favre would sign with Minnesota if he was released, Thompson immediately ratcheted up trade talks with other teams. Fearful of what might potentially turn into a soap opera, Thompson knew he couldn't trade him to an NFC team that played in Green Bay that season. As such, his choices were limited. Finally, on August 7, the Packers dealt Favre to the New York Jets for a conditional fourth-round draft pick. (The pick traded for Favre turned into a third-round selection since he played in at least 50 percent of the plays that season; it would have been a second-rounder if he played in 70 percent of the plays and the Jets qualified for the playoffs [he did, but they didn't], and a first-round pick if he played in 80 percent of the plays and the Jets made it to the Super Bowl.)

Packers fans everywhere were astonished to see Favre wearing another uniform. It was green,

> *Mark Murphy reportedly offered Favre a $25 million lifetime marketing agreement to represent the Packers in an official capacity and, more important, to* remain retired.

but not Packers Green. Although they were upset that Thompson and Favre couldn't ultimately come to terms, they knew that Favre going to the Jets was way better than Favre going to the Vikings. Incidentally, just to make sure the Jets didn't pull an end-around and immediately trade Favre to the Vikings, Thompson inserted a "poison pill" into his contract, which stipulated that the Jets would then have to give the Packers a whopping three future first-round picks—a value worth upward of $100 million.

The media spotlight shined brightly on Favre when he arrived in the Big Apple, as the team was now being referred to as the "New York

Bretts." He would be reporting to training camp extremely late and, once there, would find himself behind the eight ball in terms of understanding the Jets' offense—which was completely different than Green Bay's, or as he put it, "like learning a foreign language." The Jets, who had released quarterback Chad Pennington to make room for Favre, knew that signing him was going to be a gamble. Favre struggled at first but eventually settled into a groove. Things looked good early on in Week 4 of the season when he threw for six touchdown passes in a 56–35 win over the Arizona Cardinals. By November the Jets were the hottest team in the AFC, having won five straight to improve to 8–3. The move for Favre appeared to be paying off.

> "If Joe Montana could get traded, as great as he is, then it could happen to anyone. I never thought that could happen to me, but I am proof positive that it can."
> —Brett Favre (2008)

Then, for whatever reason, the team started to struggle in early December. Favre's throws weren't quite as crisp as before, and the team started to tank. Before long the Jets players started to snap, starting with high-profile receiver Laveranues Coles, who said of Favre, "He's the big name, he's the Hall of Famer, he's going to get the majority of the credit, but most of the guys who deserve the credit don't really get it." Favre struggled mightily down the stretch, throwing nine interceptions in the final five games. Ultimately, the team, which was a lock for the playoffs early on, wound up missing the postseason altogether in what was later hailed as a "colossal collapse."

After losing to Miami in the season finale, Jets running back Thomas Jones ripped Favre openly in the media about his decision to start the game and (indirectly) keep his consecutive-games streak alive: "You throw [three] interceptions, I'm [ticked] off, I don't like it. You know what I'm saying? I don't like it, I know everybody else on the team doesn't like it. If somebody is not playing well, they need

to come out of the game. You're jeopardizing the whole team because you're having a bad day. To me, that's not fair to everybody else. You're not the only one on the team. You're playing to win, you're playing for the Super Bowl. That's what you do all this work for.... So when you get to the wire and somebody is just giving the game up, I mean, it's just not [fair]."

Following the season Favre decided to retire yet again. It would later come out that he had a partially torn biceps tendon, an ailment that he knew

> *"Vince Lombardi went to the Washington Redskins when he left, and his name is on the [Super Bowl] trophy.... I don't hear too many people say, 'That damn traitor, he went to Washington.'"*
> *—Brett Favre (2008)*

about but that never got reported. (Incidentally, the NFL later fined the Jets $75,000, retroactively, for not adhering to the league's injury-report policy.) Favre, being the warrior that he is, played through the pain and just dealt with it. In retrospect, however, Favre would later admit that the tendon was a big factor in why the second half of his season was so abysmal. He also said that he would have been fine sitting down that season, thus ending his consecutive-starts streak.

"Absolutely, I was receptive to it last year," he told the *Star Tribune*'s Judd Zulgad in September 2009. "When we finally did an MRI and found out I had a torn biceps last year, I felt like, with about four or five games left, that even though I was making some pretty good

> *Just to make sure the Jets didn't pull an end-around and immediately trade Favre to the Vikings, Thompson inserted a "poison pill" into his contract.*

throws and some decent plays, I felt like I was doing the team more harm because I was missing on some throws.... [But we thought] that it was best to just...finish it out."

I LOVE BRETT FAVRE

Assuming that Favre had retired for good this time, the Jets moved way up and selected USC quarterback Mark Sanchez with the fifth overall pick of the 2009 draft. Shortly thereafter, the Jets officially released Favre. Favre did have one year remaining on his contract, but they released him from the reserve-retired list on April 28, renouncing all rights—meaning if he ever did sign with Minnesota that Green Bay would not receive any compensation. Asked of Favre's future, his longtime agent Bus Cook told the *USA Today*'s Jarrett Bell, "He's retired, working on his farm in Mississippi," and that as far as he was concerned, "you could stick a fork in him [he's done]."

> *"He's retired, working on his farm in Mississippi...you could stick a fork in him [he's done]."*
> —Bus Cook (2009)

From there, Favre laid low for a few months. Then, in May it was reported that Favre had a meeting with Vikings coach Brad Childress to discuss the quarterback possibly unretiring again and playing for Minnesota. Rumors ran wild from there as speculation immediately swirled that Favre was going to do the unthinkable—play for Green Bay's archenemy. Later that month Favre went in to have arthroscopic surgery on his right biceps tendon. It would be imperative to have the procedure done in order for him to return.

On June 16 Favre finally spoke publicly when he appeared as a guest on the debut episode of the *Joe Buck Live* show on HBO. There, when asked if he intended to play in '09, Favre replied, "Maybe." But later, as he was finishing a thought about the talent on the Vikings roster, he slipped and said, "*We* should be pretty good." He later explained why going to Minnesota would be a good fit. "It makes perfect sense as far as coming back because it's an offense I ran for 16 years," he said. "I can teach that offense." Later, when asked about how he thought the Packers fans would react to him running onto Lambeau Field wearing purple, Favre replied, "I don't know what to tell them. Vince Lombardi went to the Washington Redskins when

he left, and his name is on the [Super Bowl] trophy. We give that trophy out every year, and I don't hear too many people say, 'That damn traitor, he went to Washington.' Time heals a lot of things."

Talks between Favre and the Vikings heated up from there. Meanwhile, Favre continued to work out and practice with the kids at Hattiesburg High School, near his home in Mississippi. On July 16 it was reported that Vikings offensive coordinator Darrell Bevell visited Favre to watch him work out and check on the status of his newly repaired biceps tendon. Childress, meanwhile, told KFAN radio's Mike Morris that, amid all the speculation, there was in fact no deadline for Favre to come to Minnesota for organized team activities (OTAs). "My opinion is that he was a great player," said Childress. "He obviously had a setback last year. He was playing very well early. I'm anxious to see just exactly what he's got left in that cannon because he had a pretty good arm, as we know."

When asked if he intended to play in '09, Favre replied, "Maybe." But later, as he was finishing a thought about the talent on the Vikings roster, he slipped and said, "We should be pretty good."

The comments sent Vikings fans through the roof with excitement. While many got excited about the possibility of the team finally having a legitimate deep-threat quarterback, others were sickened by the mere thought of "Favre the Packer" wearing purple. With training camp in Mankato fast approaching, rumors of "will he or won't he?" consumed the airwaves as well as the blogosphere of the Gopher State like nothing anybody had ever seen before. Finally, on July 28, and after much deliberation, Favre called Childress to tell him that he wouldn't be coming out of retirement after all to play for the Vikings. It was as if a bubble the size of Paul Bunyan had been burst.

"It was the hardest decision I've ever made," Favre told ESPN. "I didn't feel like physically I could play at a level that was acceptable.

I would like to thank everyone, including the Packers, Jets, and Vikings—but, most importantly, the fans." He added, "I had to be careful not to commit for the wrong reasons. They were telling me, 'You went through all this, you had the surgery, and you've got to finish it off.' But I have legitimate reasons for my decision. I'm 39 with a lot of sacks to my name."

> The Vikings opened training camp with all the enthusiasm of a major home appliance. The media had been so excited and so jacked up about Favre's arrival that when it all fell apart at the 11th hour, nobody knew quite what to do.

From there, the Vikings opened training camp with all the enthusiasm of a major home appliance. The media had been so excited and so jacked up about Favre's arrival that when it all fell apart at the 11th hour, nobody knew quite what to do. Reporters, national media, and paparazzi alike were just standing around waiting for a story that was never going to happen. It was truly a surreal moment. Finally, Childress addressed the issue with a short prepared statement: "It was a rare and unique opportunity to consider adding not only a future Hall of Fame quarterback but one that is very familiar with our system and division. That does not detract from the team that we have."

The players and coaches worked past all the questions and hoopla and eventually got down to the business of playing football. The team wrapped up its training camp and then headed out to Indianapolis to play its first preseason game on August 14. There, behind quarterback Sage Rosenfels, whom the team had acquired in a trade from Houston during the off-season, the Vikings beat the Colts 13–3. Things were looking good. The combination of Sage and the previous year's starter, Tarvaris Jackson, was going to be a fine fit for this team, after all. Who needs Brett Favre, anyway?

Four days later and three weeks after announcing that he would stay retired, Favre shocked the sports world by announcing that he

was unretiring again and going to be signing with the Vikings. Apparently, Childress had called Favre the day before and caught him on the phone as he was heading to work out with the high school kids. Childress wanted to call one last time, to make sure that Favre's mind truly was made up. It turned out it wasn't. With that, the two started talking, and *allegedly* one thing led to another. Team owner Zygi Wilf immediately flew his jet down to Mississippi to pick up Brett and Deanna to fly them back to the Twin Cities.

"Things moved pretty quickly," Wilf told *Sports Illustrated*'s Steve Aschburner. "When Brad called us, and we spoke about it, we felt the same way: this was a small window, and we wanted to take that opportunity to make our team better. We just didn't want to worry about the future and say, 'What if?' Life is too short. We're just very excited for everybody here in Minnesota, for our fans. We're trying our best to repeat as division champs and move on to better things."

When they arrived at the airport, the media was out in full force. Favre eventually got into Childress' SUV, and together they headed out to the team's practice facility in Eden Prairie. As they drove, a TV news helicopter captured the entire event as it unfolded and broadcast it live for all to see. It was truly a spectacle. It would later be described in an eerily similar fashion to O.J. Simpson's now-infamous "low-speed" chase, except instead of driving a white Bronco, Childress was driving a black Cadillac Escalade.

ESPN's Kevin Seifert called the entire saga the "Three Bs: a Blatant, Brazen, and Brilliant ploy to skip training camp and still be given the reins to a Super Bowl–caliber team."

When the two finally got to the team's headquarters, hoards of adoring fans—some wearing No. 4 purple Vikings jerseys— had lined the streets to catch a glimpse of their newest Viking. Amid the cheers of a rock star coming on stage, Favre then went inside to make it official. There, he promptly signed a $25 million contract which guaranteed him $12 million in 2009 and $13 million in 2010,

Brett Favre gets a ride from the airport to Vikings headquarters from head coach Brad Childress on August 18, 2009, prior to signing with the team.

and contained no performance bonuses. Not bad. The guy turns down $25 million from the Packers to be their cheerleader for 20 years and gets the same cash from Minnesota—only here he has to play for just two seasons.

Incredibly, Favre then threw on a uniform and went out and practiced with his new teammates. Amazing—just a few hours after getting off the plane at 11:30 AM, he was now throwing passes and handing balls off to Adrian Peterson. When Favre introduced himself to his teammates, he kept it light: "I'm Brett from Hattiesburg,

Mississippi, and I'm the only guy on the team born in the '60s." Reserve quarterback John David Booty, who grew up idolizing Favre, even gave him the No. 4. jersey off his back and gladly made the switch to No. 9. The sight of Favre wearing a purple helmet was almost straight out of a science-fiction movie. Nobody could believe it. Packers fans were beside themselves; this was the ultimate stab in the back, in their eyes.

The media swarmed the team's practice facility as Favre mania came to a fever pitch. After his workout, he addressed the masses for the first time as a Viking. The first question everybody wanted to ask was, "Why Minnesota?"

"Everyone I've talked to—players, coaches, just people in general—said, 'If you were to go back, this is a perfect fit.' It really is," said Favre. "There's no guarantees, but [we] have a really good football team here, have a very good running game, and from my standpoint, I felt like all along I could offer some experience and leadership.... I have to admit, after I said no three weeks ago, at times I was okay with it, other times I said, 'Boy, I really felt like I could help that team.' ... As a player, regardless of sport, you've got to feel like you can make a difference, and I truly feel like I can. I just didn't want to look back [with regret].

> *"I'm Brett from Hattiesburg, Mississippi, and I'm the only guy on the team born in the '60s."*
> —Brett Favre (2009)

I have no idea how I'll feel a year from now, five years from now, 10 years from now. I didn't want to say, you know, 'What if?'"

Favre would later reveal that he had a tear in his right rotator cuff, but that he had been reassured by doctors—including Dr. James Andrews, the surgeon who repaired Favre's torn biceps muscle—that the injury was old and that he had been playing with it for quite some time. None of that seemed to matter. The reward far outweighed the risk. The Vikings had got their guy, the "missing piece to the puzzle," and the fans were ecstatic. Many would hypothesize that it was all just

a clever ruse, a smokescreen, a ploy by Favre to get out of practice time down in Mankato. We'll never know. ESPN's Kevin Seifert called the entire saga the "Three Bs: a Blatant, Brazen, and Brilliant ploy to skip training camp and still be given the reins to a Super Bowl–caliber team."

From there, Favre went about the business of learning the team's offense. He even told "Chilly," the nickname he has for Childress, that he wanted to play in the team's next preseason game against Kansas City just four days later. Unbelievable. I will never forget the moment I saw Favre running out onto the Metrodome turf wearing the purple No. 4. It was the first time any of us had actually seen it because all week he been wearing a red practice jersey. I was up at my Uncle Hank and Aunt Millie's cabin in northern Minnesota, on Lake Nichols. They were having a big party, and everybody huddled into the living room to watch the game. Never has a preseason game had so much meaning and interest. Favre played a whopping two series, completed one pass, and managed to get sacked so badly on a blitz that he later thought he'd cracked a rib.

> Favre got real serious and looked straight into the eyes of his rookie center, John Sullivan, and said, "I need you to do one thing...smile."

According to tight end Visanthe Shiancoe, in his first huddle Favre got real serious and looked straight into the eyes of his rookie center, John Sullivan, and said, "I need you to do one thing… smile." It loosened everybody up and set the tone for how Favre was going to be going about his business out on the football field. Nobody cared that Favre didn't look that good on day one. Nobody cared because what Brett Favre represented to them was hope. This team was all about winning right now, not in the future when all the veteran players get older and all the salary cap constraints become an issue, and Favre knew that. He also knew that if he was going to have success, that it was going to take time to build chemistry with his new teammates.

"Chemistry is so important," he told the *Star Tribune*'s Kevin Seifert. "I don't care how good of a player I may be or the next guy may be. In this game of football, it takes 11 [players]. Being on the same page, the unit that plays more as one than as opposed to a bunch of individuals is the one that succeeds.… You can't coach chemistry. You can't fake it. It has to happen."

Favre played well into the third quarter of the team's next preseason game, against the Texans in Houston. It was a Monday night game, and the interest was so great that it actually set a record for viewership that evening. Favre played well, too, leading the team to a victory and showing Minnesota fans that he still knew how to run a two-minute drill. On one play in particular, Favre showed everyone that he still had some gas left in the tank. Lining up at receiver in Minnesota's version of the wildcat offense, rookie receiver Percy Harvin took the snap and ran around the left end in Favre's direction. Despite playing with a banged-up rib, Favre acted as his lead blocker and even threw his body at Houston defensive back Eugene Wilson's legs to cut him down. Wilson went down in a heap, wincing in pain. While it looked good on TV, in reality it was an illegal crackback block that ultimately cost Favre a $10,000 fine from the NFL. The controver-

> *Favre played a whopping two series, completed one pass, and managed to get sacked so badly on a blitz that he later thought he'd cracked a rib.*

sial play caused an uproar throughout the media. Favre, who later apologized to Wilson, said of the incident, "I will be 40 years old in October and was weed-eating 13 days ago. I wasn't thinking about throwing blocks."

Before long Favre's No. 4 Vikings jersey shot up to No. 1 in sales at NFLShop.com, surpassing the jerseys of Bears quarterback Jay Cutler, Steelers safety Troy Polamalu, Eagles quarterback Michael Vick, and Steelers quarterback Ben Roethlisberger. Favre sat out the next preseason game but geared up to start the regular-season opener in

> *To watch him throw his first touchdown pass, a six-yarder to Percy Harvin midway through the third quarter, it looked like the weight of the world was off his shoulders. He leaped into the air in exuberation and then sprinted down into the end zone and literally tackled Harvin, knocking him on his butt.*

Cleveland against the Browns. He didn't make any promises, though.

"I may not finish the year," Favre told the *Star Tribune*'s Judd Zulgad. "If you would have asked me my first year if I would finish, I'd said I may not. No one thought I'd play 18 straight years without missing a game, me included. I have no idea what's going to happen. None. And that's an opinion. I have my opinions, as we all do, good or bad. As I said when I came in here, it's a great opportunity. I knew that from day one. When Brad called the last time, it was like, 'There's no guarantees.'"

On September 13 Favre hit the field for the first time as an official Viking. The guy looked good, not great, and definitely had some mobility issues as evidenced by the fact that he got sacked four times. He got the job done, though, and managed the offense. And to watch him throw his first touchdown pass, a six-yarder to Percy Harvin midway through the third quarter, it looked like the weight of the world was off his shoulders. He leaped into the air in exuberation and then sprinted down into the end zone and literally tackled Harvin, knocking him on his butt. He then jogged back to the sideline for a round of high fives from his new teammates. What made it so great was that he was smiling and laughing the entire way. By the way, Harvin was three years old when Favre played in his first NFL game. In all, Favre completed 14 of 21 passes for 110 yards, with one touchdown—the 465th of his career. More important, though, the Vikings won 34–20.

"I had a blast," Favre told Zulgad, after making his 270th consecutive regular-season start. "It wasn't a 400-yard passing game, but it

Brett Favre hugs wide receiver Percy Harvin in the end zone after throwing his first TD pass as a Minnesota Viking in a 34–20 win over the Cleveland Browns on opening day, September 13, 2009.

doesn't have to be. I'll be the first to tell you that. I'll take that any day of the week, as long as we win. That's what it's all about." He added, "It's a risk/reward thing against us. If you're playing against us, you're going to say, 'Are they going to throw 40 times a game or hand it to Adrian 40 or whatever times?'"

Oh, yeah, Adrian Peterson also rushed for 180 yards and three touchdowns on 25 carries, as well. That stat may be the most important of all in this entire equation, as that was a big draw for Favre in coming to Minnesota—the fact that all he had to do was hand the ball off to No. 28 and let him do his thing. The threat of Favre being able to throw deep will keep opposing defenses honest, whereas in years past, this team never had that. As such, they were able to stack eight defenders on the line to stop Peterson—widely considered to be the best running back in football. No more.

> "[Favre] played for years with injuries that would have hospitalized Godzilla."
> —Jim Klobuchar

That small intangible is one of the big reasons this team shelled out $25 million to get this guy. Stay tuned, it's going to be a hell of a ride…

Okay, So Why Do I Love Brett Favre?

For starters, I love Brett Favre because the guy is a gamer. He's old-school to the bone. Love him or hate him, you can't argue with how tough he is. His ability to play through pain is simply amazing. He's an iron man, no question. The fact that he has now started more consecutive games than any player in NFL history, recently surpassing Vikings defensive end Jim Marshall's all-time record of 270—the equivalent of Cal Ripken Jr. in baseball—is mind-boggling. A defensive lineman can play with a handful of broken fingers, whereas a quarterback can get sidelined for something as small as a bad hangnail or sore pinkie. As noted scribe Jim Klobuchar put it, "[Favre] played for years with injuries that would have hospitalized Godzilla."

I love the fact that the guy is a winner. He has won more games than any other quarterback in NFL history. Plus he holds virtually every NFL passing record and is the only three-time MVP winner. For my money, I would say he is the greatest quarterback of all time. It's not even close. As controversial and polarizing a figure as he is, I

have to give it to him. He is the perfect amalgam of all the great ones: he can scramble; he can improvise; he can throw it deep; he can read defenses maybe better than anybody; and he is deadly come the two-minute warning. How many fourth-quarter comebacks has the guy led in his career? Too many to count.

I love how the guy is fearless, both in football and in life. He's never been afraid of success, failure, praise, or criticism. He wants to play and win so badly that he really doesn't care about his legacy the way others do. How empowering is that? It's *his* career, *his* body, and *his* legacy. No matter what happens in Minnesota, he is still going to end up in Canton as a member of the Hall of Fame. Guaranteed. That's pretty cool in my book.

I love how he genuinely looks like he is having fun out there. I love watching him smile and run down the field like a little kid whenever he throws a touchdown. It's real. It's raw. It brings us all back to when we played out in the backyard with our brothers and the neighbor kids, just for the love of the game. Perhaps Klobuchar put it best when he said of Favre, "He's a football lifer. He is eternal youth, or as close to one as we're going to get, a Huckleberry Finn who became a millionaire playing the game he learned as a kid."

> "He's a football lifer. He is eternal youth, or as close to one as we're going to get, a Huckleberry Finn who became a millionaire playing the game he learned as a kid."
> —Jim Klobuchar

I love how he is not afraid to do whatever the hell he wants to do out on the field. Because he has earned the respect of his peers and coaches alike, he is able to do things others simply wouldn't fathom. From calling audibles at his discretion up at the line of scrimmage if he sees the slightest tilt of a safety or minor adjustment by a lineman, to drawing up plays on the fly, to throwing trick-play shovel passes and naked bootlegs—this guy reeks of creativity and personality. In a sports world that is all about

Brett Favre's Top 10 Career Moments
(As Determined by ESPN.com*)

1. SUPER BOWL XXXI
DATE: January 26, 1997
SCORE: Packers 35, Patriots 21
WHY IT MATTERED: Favre passed
for two touchdowns (54 and 81
yards)—including one on the
second play of the game—and ran
for another in the Packers' first
Super Bowl in 29 years.

2. PLAYING FOR HIS FATHER
DATE: December 22, 2003
SCORE: Packers 41, Raiders 7
WHY IT MATTERED: Just one day
after the sudden death of his
father, Irv, Favre passed for 399
yards and four touchdowns on
Monday Night Football in a
blowout win.

3. THE LEGEND BEGINS
DATE: September 20, 1992
SCORE: Packers 24, Bengals 23
WHY IT MATTERED: Favre joined
Green Bay prior to the season and
played in mop-up duty the week
before as the Pack fell to 0–2. This
day, he came off the bench to
replace an injured Don Majkowski
and threw the game-winning TD
pass to Kitrick Taylor with 13
seconds remaining.

4. RECORD BREAKING
DATE: September 30, 2007
SCORE: Packers 23, Vikings 16
WHY IT MATTERED: In his former
house of horrors (the Metrodome),
Favre threw a pair of touchdown
passes—his first being the 421st
of his career, making him the NFL's
all-time leader in that category.

5. PLAYOFF-BOUND
DATE: December 18, 1994
SCORE: Packers 21, Falcons 17
WHY IT MATTERED: Favre
orchestrated a final drive, capped
off when he ran for the game-
winning touchdown with 14
seconds left against the Falcons
to keep the Packers' playoff hopes
alive. Green Bay ended up making
the playoffs for the second
straight season.

6. NFC WILD-CARD
DATE: January 8, 1994
SCORE: Packers 28, Lions 24
WHY IT MATTERED: Trailing 24–21
in Detroit, Favre threw a 40-yard
touchdown pass to Sterling
Sharpe with 55 seconds left for
the Packers' first playoff win in
11 years. *continues*

7. TYING MARINO

DATE: September 23, 2007

SCORE: Packers 31, Chargers 24

WHY IT MATTERED: With the Packers trailing by four points late in the fourth quarter, Favre threw a 57-yard TD pass to Greg Jennings for the go-ahead score. It was the 420th touchdown pass in Favre's career, tying Dan Marino for the all-time record.

8. MEDICAL MARVEL

DATE: December 24, 1995

SCORE: Packers 24, Steelers 19

WHY IT MATTERED: In a game the Packers needed to win to win the NFC Central, Favre, the victim of a crushing hit, came back after coughing up blood to throw a touchdown pass to tight end Mark Chmura.

9. MVP-BOUND

DATE: November 12, 1995

SCORE: Packers 35, Bears 28

WHY IT MATTERED: Favre returned just one week after severely spraining his ankle to toss for 336 yards and a career-high five touchdown passes at Lambeau Field. He would go on to win his first MVP that season.

10. MNF MIRACLE

DATE: September 11, 1995

SCORE: Packers 27, Bears 24

WHY IT MATTERED: At Soldier Field in Chicago, Favre tied an NFL record with a 99-yard touchdown pass to Robert Brooks in the second quarter on *Monday Night Football*—and finished the game with 312 yards passing and three touchdowns.

*ESPN Research, August 19, 2009

the bottom line, Brett Favre has enough screw-you cash to not care about the money at this point in his career. He lives by his own set of rules, the "Brett Rules." As such, he is able to play in a way that is fun for him—even if that means skipping training camp and pissing a few people off. That freedom—to do what we want, on our own terms— is something we should all strive for in life.

Beyond all that, I love Brett Favre because he gives my team an aura of hope—both on and off the field. I have struggled with this team ever since I can remember. The pain runs deep. This franchise is 0–4 in Super Bowls, and let's face it, we're desperate. So, if Brett Favre wants

Brett Favre celebrates an Adrian Peterson touchdown run in the first half against the Cleveland Browns on September 13, 2009, his first regular-season game in a Vikings uniform.

Photo courtesy of Getty Images

to come play for my team to help us win a Super Bowl, then why wouldn't I love Brett Favre? Sure, he is old, but the guy can still bring it. And if he is somehow able to lead us to the promised land and deliver a championship, then that will mean we will have a much better chance of getting a new stadium for this team. And if that happens, then I will *really* love Brett Favre.

What people around the country don't realize about this story is that we need a new stadium in Minnesota in a big way. I think signing Favre was an "all-in" kind of move. The lease is up at the Metrodome in 2011, and after that, to the best of my

> *Ed Roski...is on the prowl to buy controlling interest in a team with stadium issues. Well, we've got issues. If we don't find a resolution to those issues, we may all be rooting for the Los Angeles Vikings.*

knowledge, the team would be free and clear to move to Los Angeles, if they so desired. Don't think it couldn't happen. It happened with the Minneapolis Lakers, back in 1960 when they got hijacked to L.A.—so anything is possible.

If Favre can help the Vikings win now, our chances of keeping this team in Minnesota greatly improve. Maybe it wouldn't be enough to get a new stadium built, but it might just be enough to prevent the team from leaving, and enough to at least raise the resources to fix up the Metrodome. (Talk about putting lipstick on a pig…) The clock is ticking on this whole thing, though, and I, for one, am nervous.

Billionaire financier Ed Roski is building a new stadium in the City of Industry, outside Los Angeles, and is on the prowl to buy controlling interest in a team with stadium issues. Well, we've got issues. If we don't find a resolution to those issues, we may all be rooting for the Los Angeles Vikings. And, *no*, that does not have a nice ring to it.

But the Vikings ownership group, led by the Wilf family, has been outstanding. They have spared no expense in upgrading this team and are committed to winning a Super Bowl. They have opened their

wallets at every turn and signed a handful of big-time free agents, including Jared Allen, Antoine Winfield, and of course Favre. For that, Minnesota fans should be grateful. Let's just hope that in the final hour they can find a way to get something done. Whatever the solution, we need momentum, and that all starts with No. 4. The way I see it, this is a classic "use-use" relationship: Favre will use the Vikings to exact revenge on Ted Thompson, and the Vikings will use Favre to win a Super Bowl (and get a new sta-

> The last, yet perhaps most important, reason why I love Brett Favre: he wants to crush the Packers this season! Come on, what's not to love about that?

dium). If you're a Vikings fan, that use-use is a win-win. It's beautiful, and it leads to the last, yet perhaps most important, reason why I love Brett Favre: he wants to crush the Packers this season! Come on, what's not to love about that?

As you can see, there are many reasons for loving Brett Favre. No, not the "man crush" kind of love, the "I'm a desperate die-hard lifelong Vikings fan" kind of amour. Now, if you want to know my reasons for hating Brett Favre, you'll have to flip the book, because there are definitely two sides to this guy.

Here is what some players, media, and fans have to say about loving Brett Favre.

Players Love Brett Favre

Pete Bercich

Former Vikings Linebacker and Assistant Coach,
Current Vikings Radio Analyst

As for the signing of Brett, all I can say is wow, it is amazing what's riding on one man this season. Expectations are running high in Minnesota, that is for sure. The stars aligned for us to get him, without a doubt. From a football standpoint, he is a great fit for this team. He is comfortable with the coaching staff and knows this system. Plus, he doesn't have to do it all. In Minnesota Brett Favre isn't the entire offense. This is Adrian Peterson's offense, plain and simple. Brett is here to hand him the ball and to keep the defenses honest. We never had that before, and now that he is behind center, teams can't stack the box against us. He changes everything for us, everything.

With regards to the "Favre Rules," I am sure some of the guys in the locker room are not completely thrilled with the way he is handled. But he has earned that, and the players know it. I remember when I was coaching with the team, Chuck Knox Sr. said at a team meeting one time, "Some of you have to follow rules, and some of you have to follow guidelines." He was basically saying that not all players

were going to be treated equally. For a guy like me, a special-teamer who was always trying to crack the starting lineup—I showed up for seven years and never showed up late for a meeting once. Hey, I knew that they could cut me and find somebody else to do my job pretty easily. I followed the rules. But guys like Cris Carter, Randy Moss, and Robert Smith—those guys followed guidelines. They knew that they weren't going to get cut, so they did things that they knew they could get away with. Players need to know their roles within the team and understand who's who and what's what. Obviously, Brett Favre has very lenient "guidelines" to follow.

> "The guy can read defenses and make adjustments in a heartbeat. He knows where he will have one-on-one coverage, and nine times out of 10 he will beat you. The guy is amazing that way. Defenses fear him, they really do."
> —Pete Bercich

Now, if he started bitching about players publicly and trying to play the role of general manager, too, then guys would get pissed. But that is not going to happen, because Brett is a professional and he has been around this game for a long, long time. The bottom line is this: if you are going to go ahead and have separate rules for separate players, then you better win. Because at the end of the day, players will tolerate just about anything as long as they are winning. When the team is winning, everybody is fat and happy. If the team starts losing, then watch out. That's when the finger-pointing starts and the wheels can start to fall off. I think that is exactly what happened in New York with the Jets last year. Nobody complained early on when the team was winning, but then when Brett got hurt and they started losing—all of a sudden you heard grumblings from the locker room. Now all of a sudden you have a guy who isn't playing very well and has all of these special guidelines on top of that. It wasn't long before guys started throwing other guys under the bus, and before you knew it, all hell broke loose.

Look, players hate training camp. All of them. None of those guys want to be there, and if they tell you differently, they are lying. It is something that they know they have to do, though, so they suck it up and make the best of it. Every year around training camp, you look at the bank statement and ask yourself the same question: why am I doing this? That is a gut-check time that all players go through because nobody wants to go through two-a-days and live in a dorm. No way. We do it because we love to play the game and because we love to get paid. Period. So I understand why Brett didn't want to go to camp, sure. Do I agree with it? That is not my call. I am just glad he is wearing purple and that we figured out a way to get him here. The bottom line is this: we are a better football team with Brett Favre versus without Brett Favre.

All the players in the locker room are totally on board with Brett. They know that he is a good player who works hard and that he wants to win. That is all they care about—winning. They want to win, and if he can help them achieve that goal, then it's all good. Brett will mentor the younger players and make everybody on that team better. They will listen to him because he has been to war before and he has won the ultimate prize. A lot of the guys are in awe of him because the guy is a legend. He really is. He understands how to get the most out of his teammates, too, especially the receivers. He uses their strengths to his advantage and puts them in positions to thrive. He is so smart, too. The guy can read defenses and make adjustments in a heartbeat. He knows where he will have one-on-one coverage, and nine times out of 10 he will beat you. The guy is amazing that way. Defenses fear him, they really do.

I can tell you, as a former player who used to beat his head against the wall trying to get to Brett Favre, that the only way to beat him is to hit him and knock him down. You have to roll the dice. I remember one year when we beat Green Bay in a playoff game, it was because one of our linebackers, Chris Claiborne, blitzed him, and the first thing that hit the ground was his helmet. He threw three interceptions after that and should have thrown five. That is his only weakness,

that's it. You have to gamble with him and send guys who will hopefully get to him. The problem with that, though, is that once you blitz,
he is the best at picking that stuff up and making you pay. He can audible at the line and find the open guy. He will find your weaknesses and
exploit them. The guy is really smart that way, and he will burn you
time and time again. You can't sit back and play coverage against him,
either, because he will figure you out and pick you apart. You have to
hit him, you have to get him on the ground, and you have to rough him
up. You have to get him throwing for his life, or else he will kill you.

As for the rivalry between the Packers and Vikings, it is huge. Look,
I am a Chicago native, so I understand how much the Bears fans hated
the Packers, but it isn't even close to how much Vikings fans hate
them. I played in Minnesota and live here now, and it is really intense.
The problem we have here is that all of these people grow up in the
middle of nowhere in Wisconsin, they go to college, and then they
need to get a real job—so they move to Minnesota. Then some dip-
shit moves in next door to you and flies a Packer flag on Sunday. What
the hell is up with that? That drives me freaking crazy. Talk about
annoying. Think about this, we are the *only* market in the country
where we have a two-hour radio show on our sports talk radio station
that is dedicated solely to our archrival: *Packer Preview*. When I was a
player here with the Vikings, that drove me absolutely nuts. Stuff like
that just fuels this rivalry, though—which, in my opinion, just makes
football season that much more fun.

Greg Coleman
Former Vikings Punter and Current NFL Radio/TV Analyst
There are several different perspectives in looking at the Favre
signing. First, from a fan's perspective, it is all about winning. They
just want to win. They don't care how their team wins, or with whom
they win, they just want to win. So I don't think Minnesota fans care
about Brett Favre wearing purple. Heck, if Johnny Lujack came back
from the dead to play quarterback for this team, they would welcome
him, too. They are enjoying the fact that so many Packer fans are so

up in arms about the whole thing, which I think is actually pretty funny.

Second, from the organization's standpoint, it's about winning right now. In their eyes, all of the pieces are finally in place. They went all out and really made a play to get [Favre] and they have big expectations. They hope that he will indeed be that missing piece of the puzzle that will ultimately lead the team to a Super Bowl. On paper that all looks good. It is on the field where it really matters, though. They need to stay healthy, or like me, they too will wind up on the sideline.

> *"All of these people grow up in the middle of nowhere in Wisconsin, they go to college, and then they need to get a real job—so they move to Minnesota. Then some dipshit moves in next door to you and flies a Packer flag on Sunday."*
> *—Pete Bercich*

Lastly, from the player's perspective, some will say he is too old. As a former player, I don't see it that way. I say if he can come back and get the job done, then more power to him. Look, once this is done, it's done. That's it. Once your name comes off of everybody's board and the word goes out that you are retired, that your services are no longer available, then that means you are done. At that point, life as you know it in the National Football League is over. It is now time to enter the real world and be prepared to do something else. So, from that standpoint, I totally understand where Brett is coming from. Hey, if the Vikings offered me a contract to come back, I would take it in a heartbeat. Most of us would, because those of us who were fortunate enough to play the game at this level love to compete. We love to play the game. That is Brett Favre to a tee, he loves to play the game. And, until his body says otherwise, he will continue to play football in the NFL. I tell you what, though, that arm still looks good. No. 4 can still throw it, no question about it.

Personally, as a fan, I am thrilled Brett is a Viking. Brett is a competitor, he just loves to compete. He has so much confidence in

himself and in his abilities that he feels like there is nothing he can't accomplish out on the football field. He is one of the greatest to ever play this game, without a doubt. Professionally, however, Brett is one of 53 men on this team, and as a journalist, I will be fair. I will give him the same respect as well as the same criticism for poor play as I will for the other players. I won't criticize the person, I will only criticize his play. There is a big difference in my mind. What he does between the white lines, that is what I will focus on—not all of the other off-the-field stuff—I will leave that for the paparazzi. Sure, I may talk to him about his family and about golf, to have fun, but nothing too serious.

> "If it comes down to the last drive and you need it, people in the huddle will believe he can do it. He's been there so many times."
>
> —Steve Mariucci

Don Beebe
Former Packers Wide Receiver

The Streak: it's something as a player you just marvel at. It's hard enough to get through one season, even one game, let alone 200-plus games. On the other hand, when I think of Brett, it's not all that surprising. You would literally have to cut his legs off for him not to go out there and play.

I think they absolutely forced him to retire. They probably just told him privately that they were ready to move on with Aaron [Rodgers], which is fine, because that was a business decision. But Brett wasn't ready to retire. So now what do you do? Cut Brett Favre? That ain't going to happen, so they had to force that retirement, in my mind. It's obvious that he wasn't ready to give it up…. This is all speculation, but I think he was originally told [by the Packers], "Brett, it's time for us to move on without you," and that hurt his feelings. Okay, he was like, "Jeez, you know, look what I have done for you for 16 years and now you are going to tell me this? I was one pass away from giving you

another Super Bowl, and you are going to tell me I am out?" So that probably bruised his ego a little bit.

Steve Mariucci
Former Packers Assistant Coach and Current NFL TV Analyst
I was there when he was a baby, his first four years in Green Bay, and [now] he looks to me like he's making all the same kind of throws. It looks like his arm is sharp, fresh, and healthy. I don't know if he's feeling any pain or not, but he looks sharp. It's interesting to be able to jump right off the bus and jump right in the huddle and run this offense. It's all familiar to him…. His knowledge and experience in the system. His leadership. If it comes down to the last drive and you need it, people in the huddle will believe he can do it. He's been there so many times. He brings a lot of experience…. I just said, "Let it rip," and, "Have fun." He's not going to start second-guessing any decision. He has made a commitment to this organization and is going to go for it. I think we all know that with him, they have a pretty good chance to do some damage in this NFL chase.

Jon Gruden
Former Packers Assistant Coach and Current NFL TV Analyst
He's a great player, and he's going to help this football team in a lot more ways. He's a winner and still has a lot of talent. I tried to get Favre last year. That's probably a big reason why I'm not coaching, I didn't get him. I think it's a prefect fit for Minnesota.

Frank Winters
Former Packers Center
The most important things to Brett were the wins and winning world championships. Brett was a lead-by-example kind of a guy. He wasn't one of those rah-rah guys who would try to cheer you up and give you one of those "win one for the Gipper" speeches before the game. His presence in the locker room was unbelievable because he went out there week-in and week-out and helped to do whatever he could to

help the team win. He would show up every Sunday, play hurt, and just get the job done. He was just so well respected among his peers in the NFL.

I have known Brett a long time and I roomed with him on the road for 11 years. He has so many good qualities. He was as humble as they come. He had fun. He played to the last whistle, that was the type of player he was. He didn't care if you were Joe Schmoe or Joe Montana, either—he never thought he was better than anybody else. He treated everybody with the same amount of respect. The guys really looked up to that. He was just one of the greatest players who ever played the game. He came in the huddle week-in and week-out, winning or losing, with the same attitude. If we were winning by 21, he would want to drive down and score to make it 28. That was his mentality. He was the kind of guy who never let up.

> "I tried to get Favre last year. That's probably a big reason why I'm not coaching, I didn't get him."
> —Jon Gruden

Brett was [also] a practical jokester and really a funny individual. He loved to crack jokes and play tricks on people. I will never forget one time we were walking out together for practice and something didn't quite feel right. Well, it turned out he put Icy Hot in my jock. I had to run back and take a shower it stung so bad. Nobody was free from his pranks, either. I mean, he would get players, coaches, whoever was around.

I remember one night we were in New Orleans, down in the French Quarter for Mardis Gras. He thought Mark Chmura went into this Port-a-Potty, so I look down and see him trying to tip the thing over. I yell over to him to ask him what the hell he is doing. He says that Chmura was in there and that he was trying to tip it over. I said that Chmura wasn't in there, he was up here. He says, "No way, I saw him walk in there." All of a sudden a policeman opens the door and walks out. We started laughing so hard. Old Brett just started apologizing like

Green Bay Packers center Frank Winters protects Brett Favre as he drops back to pass during their NFC Championship Game victory over the Carolina Panthers on January 12, 1997, at Lambeau Field. *Photo courtesy of Getty Images*

crazy. "I am *so* sorry, I thought my buddy was in there!" It was pretty funny. That was Brett, though, always laughing and having fun. We had some great times together.

Doug Pederson
Former Packers Quarterback

Brett never missed a game, he was so tough, so durable. He was a great leader, too. He made other guys around him better football players and got them to elevate their game to higher standards. He was the MVP. He was excited about the wins, yet he stayed humble. The losses were tough on him, though, because he always felt like he was responsible for that. He wanted to make his team better and he wanted to make himself better. Losing just pained him. He hated to lose.

He was pretty laid back. He's a prankster, though, especially to the rookies. If you went into the restroom and had to shut the door to your stall, that was a big mistake. Brett would go get a big ice bucket full of icy cold water and pour it over the wall and just soak guys. It was always the rookies, too, because the veterans knew better. They knew that if Brett was around, then they wouldn't shut the door. It was hilarious to watch guys come out of the bathroom all soaking wet and freezing cold.

I obviously never got to start any games during my time in Green Bay as Brett's backup. That role carried over to off the field, too, I suppose. He and I used to love to hunt together. Well, I remember one time we were out deer hunting, and he had a broken thumb at the time. Sure enough, he shot a deer, and I wound up having to drag that thing out of the woods all by myself. That was what a good backup was supposed to do, I guess. He carried the rifles, and I dragged the deer for what seemed like an eternity. That was just the way it went.

A defining moment for me with Brett was when his dad passed back in 2003. We played Oakland that night, and I will never forget it. To watch him lead us to victory that game was something I will never forget. I will never experience anything like that again. To see a group of men come together for three hours in honor of Irvin Favre

was pretty special. That to me was Brett summed up. To see him in such pain, and hurting, yet to be able to perform with nearly 400 yards passing and ultimately leading us to victory was amazing. That is Brett. He would get knocked down but he always got up. He was so tough.

Mike Ditka
Hall of Fame Chicago Bears Tight End and Former Head Coach
Brett Favre is a Hall of Fame football player. He is incredibly durable and he is smart. He has that gunslinger mentality, too, where he's just not afraid to screw up. And, if he does screw up, he will come right back at you to make up for it. He doesn't dwell on his mistakes, which is a real rarity in this league. Now, is he going to be a great addition in Minnesota? Time will tell. They sure went out on a limb to get him, though, and they made some concessions to get him in there—including signing him after training camp. Times have changed. Lombardi wouldn't have allowed something like that. Neither would Tom Landry.... I think he can still play the game, though, and that is the bottom line. He is just a hell of a quarterback. When he is on his game, he can be very effective. All in all, I think his return is a good thing for football. He certainly makes it interesting, that is for sure. As for all of that revenge stuff that you hear about in the media, I think that is a bunch of bull. Look, the only thing Brett is concerned about right now is winning a Super Bowl. He went there because he thinks he is the missing piece of the puzzle and that his team can win. That's it. Period. People can speculate all they want, but the reality is this: Minnesota really wanted him and they really went out on a limb to get him. Will it pay off for them? Who knows. Either way, it is going to be one hell of a story.

Darrell Bevell
Vikings Offensive Coordinator and Former Packers Quarterbacks Coach
I think [Brett's] leadership skills speak for itself. You know, the guy, he automatically has credibility when he steps into the huddle. He'll end up having good rapport with all those guys, but I think, if you ask

> "Brett Favre is a Hall of Fame football player.... His return is a good thing for football."
>
> —Mike Ditka

some of them, the first time he stepped into the huddle, all of them were all ears, looking right at him and ready to follow him. I think every day that we'll go out there, he'll get better, he'll improve....

There are still a few things that he has to get used to, some of the things that have evolved since the time that we were together. But for the most part, about 95 percent he knows—how they come out of routes, how they shake free, what type of ball he needs to throw to them. Where he can throw it to specific guys.... I already have some history with him. I know what he can do, what he likes to do. So I think that does help.... As we go, we'll see how he fits in with our guys. Because that's the most important thing. Not exactly what he can do, but how we can blend his skills with the team.

Bill Romanowski
Former Pro Bowl Linebacker

What makes Brett so good is that he plays quarterback like a linebacker. You would hit him, and he would say, "Hit me a little harder next time, Romo...." The guy is just plain tough. We played against each other for a lot of years, and I had a lot of respect for him. I remember blitzing him one time back in '94 when I was with Philadelphia, it was my first sack as an Eagle. I hit him pretty good. Then, afterward, I jumped up and got in his face to try to intimidate him. I screamed, "I'm gonna kill you! You're goin' down!" He just looked at me and started laughing. I was like, "What the hell is this?" I knew right then and there that you couldn't get into his head, no way. Mentally, he is as tough as they come. To see him smile like that, though, it was like, "Okay, game on!"

I went up against him in the Super Bowl in '98, as well, and he gave our defense everything we could handle. They were the defending champs and had just a great team. We were very fortunate to win that

game, it was a real battle. Brett hates to lose and he went down swinging. As a defense, we took the approach of not blitzing him. We played cover-three against him and had success. As soon as you started bringing blitzes on him, he was able to take the game into his own hands. When he got flushed out of the pocket, that was when you really started to get nervous. That was when he was at his best, when he could be creative and improvise.

He just has an amazing ability to make plays. Whether it was off his back foot or with his opposite hand, he was just amazing at making things happen. It was a gift. He is a very intelligent player. He also had the ability to bounce back, to shake off bad plays. Unlike most quarterbacks, if he throws an interception, he comes right back at you. It pisses him off, and he comes

> *"I jumped up and got in his face to try to intimidate him. I screamed, 'I'm gonna kill you! You're goin' down!' He just looked at me and started laughing. I was like, 'What the hell is this?'"*
> *—Bill Romanowski*

back even harder. If he gets nailed, so be it. He gets right back up and smiles. God, he is such a competitor.

As for Brett playing in Minnesota, I say go for it. If he is able to play the game and he is enjoying himself, god bless him. How lucky is he to be able to be in a position to go out there and compete and play the game at the age of 40? I think it is awesome. I would love to still be playing. I am jealous, to tell you the truth, I really am. Having said that, I do get tired of all the media coverage. At one point this past summer I thought that ESPN should just give him his own damn channel. I think he gets more press than the rest of the NFL combined!

Dean Dalton
Former Vikings Assistant Coach and Current TV Analyst
The first time I met Brett was back in '97, when the Packers beat New England in the Super Bowl down in New Orleans. I was working as

an assistant coach at the time but was in town to watch the big game. That night, after the Packers won the game, I was out with a buddy of mine in the French Quarter. All of a sudden this big limo pulls up amid a sea of tens of thousands of drunk fans, and out pops a whole bunch of Packers. Among them was Mark Chmura, who I knew. He sees me and says, "Hey, Deano, come on and join the party!" So we jumped in with them as the police escorted us to this private party room for friends and family in a restaurant along Bourbon Street. We go up there, and before I know it I am talking to Brett as he is explaining to me how he called the audible on the touchdown pass to Andre Rison. It was just surreal. Everybody was partying and having a great time. Eventually, Brett goes out onto the balcony overlooking Bourbon Street. Immediately, the fans start to go nuts, thousands of them. He then gets them to start chanting, "Go, Pack, Go! Go, Pack, Go!" Then, right in the middle of it, he gets them to switch the cheer to "The Bears Still Suck! The Bears Still Suck!" It was absolutely hilarious. Here is the MVP quarterback of the Super Bowl, up on a balcony all by himself leading cheers to a bunch of drunk lunatics—half of whom were wearing cheese heads. I will never forget that moment for as long as I live. I learned right then and there that there was another side to Brett Favre.

> **"Brett goes out onto the balcony overlooking Bourbon Street.... The fans start to go nuts.... He then gets them to start chanting, 'Go, Pack, Go! Go, Pack, Go!' Then, right in the middle of it, he gets them to switch the cheer to 'The Bears Still Suck! The Bears Still Suck!'"**
> **—Dean Dalton**

Everybody has an opinion on why he came here, but mine is a little more analytical. I think it was a combination of familiarity, where he knew this offense, and the reality that this team—which was built to win right now—desperately needed a quarterback. This is a very

comfortable situation for him, it really is. With regards to familiarity, he knows the coaches and he knows this version of the West Coast offense. Darrell Bevell is one of his best friends, as is Ryan Longwell, who was his kicker in Green Bay for nine seasons prior. They are golf buddies and can hang out. Beyond that, Minnesota has a pretty good offensive line, which is very important for Brett. He is 40 and doesn't want to be running for his life all season. Throw in the fact that the Vikings have arguably the best one-two punch in the league at running back this season with Adrian Peterson and Chester Taylor, and it was a no-brainer for him. He also has a really good receiving tight end, too, in Visanthe Shiancoe, who has really come of age as of late, as well as a solid blocking tight end in Jimmy Kleinsasser. He has a vertical stretch guy in Bernard Berrian, a red-zone threat in Sidney Rice, and a move-the-chains guy in Percy Harvin. Add in the top-ranked defense in the league last year, and this was looking pretty good for him.

The bottom line is that he figures he can win here. The pieces are in place for him, he doesn't have to do it all. He just has to manage the offense and keep the opposing defenses honest. Last year with the Jets, he had a good team. This year with the Vikings, he has a *very* good team. The Wilf family has made a huge investment in this team as evidenced by the fact that we have the third-highest payroll in the league. This is a championship team. No doubt about it. There is a real buzz about this group, and that all starts with No. 4. So this is a very unique opportunity for Brett, and I think he wants to go out on top, I really do....

To say that Brett is an iron man is a bit of an understatement. His durability is legendary, it really is. And he is so tough—mentally and physically—maybe the toughest ever to play the game. His consecutive-starts streak is mind-boggling. That record will *never* be broken, no way. The guy is just a machine. He gets injured, but he is somehow able to overcome them and aspire to greatness. The other quarterbacks in the league are in awe of the guy, they really are. They don't know how he can do it, game-in and game-out.

I was talking to Tony Romo recently when Dallas was in town to play the Vikings for a preseason game.... He and Brett were talking before the game, and Brett wound up giving Tony some advice, which he later shared with me. He basically told him that people were going to either love him or hate him, and that as soon as he stopped allowing that to affect him—that was when he could truly take his game to the next level. Brett talked about how he had to learn that the hard way, and that it took a long time to figure out. But once he did, it was life-changing for him. It used to really bother him when he got booed or when negative things were written about him, but now he can just blow it off and focus on winning football games. For Tony, who grew up idolizing Brett as a kid and basically [modeled] his game after him, to now be able to talk to him as a peer and share advice, it was a pretty meaningful conversation.

At the end of the day, I just love the way Brett Favre plays the game. Selfishly, though, I am especially glad he is on our side of the sidelines for a change. He has burned us so many times up here over the years, too many to count. I actually coined a phrase that a lot of coaches use in disgust which describes the act of Brett burning a cornerback on a pump fake and connecting with his receiver for a touchdown—I called it getting "Favred." Needless to say, we, as coaches, have all been "Favred" more times than we care to remember. I remember talking to Zygi Wilf shortly after Brett signed his contract. He came over all excited, smiled, and said to me, "Now it is our turn to 'Favre' the competition for a change." Not bad for a billionaire!

Ryan Longwell
Vikings Kicker and Longtime Friend of Favre

We were teammates together in Green Bay for nine years, so being reunited again is wonderful. It was an honor to play with the guy for so many years in Green Bay, and I am really excited about playing together on such a great team. I have a lot of great memories from our time together as teammates both on and off the field, and I am excited about being able to hang out with him again now that we are back on

New Viking Brett Favre and Dallas Cowboys quarterback Tony Romo talk before their teams' preseason game in the Metrodome on Friday, September 4, 2009.

the same sideline. It's always great to have a friend back, especially a guy like Brett who is someone I really enjoy being around. We spend a lot of time out on the golf course together; he is a great golfer. We used to have some great matches up in Green Bay at Oneida Country Club. Every Tuesday and Friday after practice we would head up there and duke it out on the links. It was awesome. Just to be outside and away from the game, it was almost therapeutic. You would have to shoot 4 or 5 under par to win back in those days, too—it was intense. Brett is a competitor, both on and off the field, whatever he

is doing—that is for sure. His handicap isn't what it used to be, but he can still hit it a *long* way....

As far as coming to Minnesota, we talked a lot about it prior to him coming. He wanted to know all about the Twin Cities, as far as what it was like living here, as well as about the football side of things. We also talked about what it was like going from being a Packer to a Viking, and about going from one rival to another. Now, obviously, I am much lower on the totem pole than he is, so his transition is much different than mine. It was just nice to be there for him as a friend whom he could lean on and trust. In the end, I think he made a great decision, and we are thrilled to have him here in Minnesota.

The Green Bay fans are great for their undying support of their team. We, as players, have the perspective from the business side of things, though, whereas they, as fans, have their own perspective. We just have to respect one another and sometimes agree to disagree. Coming to Minnesota from Green Bay was tough at first for me, no question. I got a lot of hate mail and was called a traitor, but that just comes with the territory when you move from one rival to another. I just wanted them to know that I wasn't choosing the Vikings over the Packers, I was choosing to take a job in my line of work. It was a great opportunity for me and my family, and I have no regrets. It has been a great career move for me, and I am excited about my future with the team, even more so now with Brett here. At the end of the day, this is a business. You can't let your emotions get too involved, or you will beat yourself up.

As for Brett dealing with all of that, I am sure he is getting it *way* more than I did. But he will be all right. It will be weird for him when he goes back to Lambeau, no doubt about it. It is just different the first time, but after a while it is just like any other game. The good news for Brett is that he had that buffer year in New York. So it's not like he came directly over the border from Wisconsin to Minnesota. It is a unique situation for him, but he'll be just fine. He's a professional.

What makes Brett so great is the fact that he plays the game with so much emotion. He goes full throttle all the time. That is just the

only way he knows how to play. There is an endearing side to that, I think. He doesn't hide behind the face mask or play the game robotically. People can relate to that. Whether its fans or teammates or coaches, they can relate to the way he plays the game. It is the way we played it as kids out in the backyard. Not only is it endearing, it is really fun to watch, as well.

The guys look up to him, he is a natural leader. He is a student of the game, too, always wanting to learn as much as he can about all the little nuances of the game. I will never forget the time he wanted to be my holder for PATs [point-after kicks]. We lined up in practice one day, and he pulled the old Lucy–Charlie Brown switcheroo on me. It was pretty funny, but needless to say he got put way down on the depth chart after that—which thrilled me. Heck, I was just nervous about kicking his hand accidentally or something and ending his streak. So I was fine with him just playing quarterback.

Beyond that, he is a great locker-room guy. He keeps everyone loose and on their toes, too. In here he can goof off and have fun, which is a side to him that the fans don't always see. In Green Bay the guy was just always pulling pranks. In Green Bay, at the old Lambeau Field, we had a ground-level hot tub, so you always had to be careful walking past it with Brett nearby because he used to love to shove guys in there when they least expected it. You had to have some thick skin, and you had to keep your head on a swivel with him around, that was for sure, because you never knew where he was going to strike from next.

> *"Ron Wolf, our GM...asks him in a really serious tone, 'Brett, I need to know, what specifically does this team need in order to get back to the Super Bowl?' Without missing a beat, Brett looks him straight in the eyes and says, 'Ron, we could really use a water softener in the shower.'"*
> —*Ryan Longwell*

I will never forget the first time I heard Brett crack a joke. It was right after the team had won the Super Bowl, and we were in the locker room along with Ron Wolf, our GM at the time. Ron asks him in a really serious tone, "Brett, I need to know, what specifically does this team need in order to get back to the Super Bowl?" Without missing a beat, Brett looks him straight in the eyes and says, "Ron, we could really use a water softener in the shower." I was a rookie at the time and didn't know if I was supposed to laugh or not, but it was hilarious.

Pat Williams
Vikings Pro Bowl Defensive Tackle
I've chased him around the field for a lot of years up until now, and I am just thrilled that we're finally on the same team. It's been fun getting to know him; he's a great locker-room guy and he's a fun guy. He fits in really well up here and we're excited to have him on the team. As for what makes him so good, he's just old-school. He's a throwback. He's a winner. He's also pretty laid back, which is nice, too. So we're excited about the season coming up and about our chances this year. With him leading the way, it could be pretty special.

John Sullivan
Vikings Center
Having Brett as a teammate is great. He's an impact player who can help this team win, and we are pretty excited to have him. Obviously, he's played for a long time, too, so he's a great resource. The guy is just a wealth of knowledge. I've learned a ton from him and just try to soak it all in whenever I'm around him. He's fun in the locker room, too, where he has already established himself as a pretty good prankster. He is always messing with people, myself included. With me, he'll walk up toward me and act like he is about to catch something. So I duck and take cover, only to realize that nothing is coming. He pretty much gets me with that every day. You'd think I would stop falling for it by now, but... oh, well.

Jared Allen
Vikings Pro Bowl Defensive End

Having Brett here is cool. The guy is a future Hall of Famer, so what more could you ask for? As a fan, you just have to appreciate and enjoy this. It's great. The whole thing has been pretty crazy, but it has all worked out. I texted him early on to see where he was at and to let him know where we were at from a team standpoint. I think he appreciated that, which was great. Brett's been playing this game for a long, long time. You have to respect that. He has a real passion for the game, and that is evident when you watch him. His willingness to study and to do the little things, that is what separates him in my mind. He works hard to be the best, and that is why he has had so much success over his career. And, once you get past the whole "Brett Favre" thing, you realize that he's really a pretty down-to-earth kind of guy. He's fun in the locker room, we laugh and joke around—it's all good. Now that the hype has died down, we're just trying to stay focused so that we can win football games. The bottom line is that he makes us a better football team, and we are happy to have him.

Sidney Rice
Vikings Wide Receiver

Playing with Brett has been really exciting so far. Being able to learn from a guy who has been around for 19 seasons and has done so much out on the football field is pretty neat. I have learned a ton from him. I ask him questions all the time about what he is seeing on certain plays. We're communicating and we're getting on the same page, which is so important. He tells us receivers what he sees on certain routes and then he tells us how he likes to throw the ball. He tries to work with our strengths, too, which is great. It is just a timing thing now, and that comes with lots of practice. He has been around and seen everything there is to see, though, as far as coverages and defensive packages, so I am just trying to take it all in. I will say this, too, he may be getting up there in years, but his arm is still there. Absolutely! He throws a *hard* ball, a nice tight spiral. I haven't broken any fingers *yet*, and hopefully I won't any time soon.

Chad Greenway
Vikings Linebacker

I grew up in South Dakota rooting for all the NFC North teams, but watching Brett Favre on TV was special. I garnered a large appreciation for the way he played the game with so much passion. So to play alongside him now is really a thrill. It has been fun having him on the team so far, and I am sure it will just continue to get better and better as we go. I am just glad that he is able to keep playing. He obviously loves the game and he feels like he can still contribute. He enjoys coming in to work on his game and he is always trying to get better. Being a relatively young guy myself, for me to see a 39-year-old veteran who wants to come in to work every day because he loves what he does, that is pretty inspiring. Hey, we're just thrilled to have him wearing purple. He is an MVP, a Super Bowl champion and a future Hall of Famer. What else can you say?

> *"He throws a hard ball, a nice tight spiral. I haven't broken any fingers yet..."*
> — *Sidney Rice*

Ben Leber
Vikings Linebacker

It is hard to put into words just what it means having Brett here. He is a great presence in the locker room and he has really fit in nicely. The fans have been coming out in droves, showing their support for him, and that has been great. Brett is a Hall of Fame player and he is a big draw. People are interested in him, and that has been really exciting for all of us. As far as the fans and the rivalry with the Packers and all of that, it is funny to see how quickly the die-hard Vikings fans embraced him. That was surprising to a lot of people, I think, because of the intense hatred between these two teams.

As a player, Brett has so much tenacity, and everybody appreciates his approach to the game. His durability speaks for itself. I mean, he hasn't ever missed a start over his 18-year career, which is beyond

amazing. Then, when you look at the things that he has gone through personally, as well as professionally—with all of the injuries—you can't help but be a little bit in awe of the guy. He is a real warrior and somehow always plays through the pain and suffering. That is what has earned him the respect of the guys in the locker room. We are just excited about the fact that he is on our side. I am sure that doesn't sit well with the Wisconsin fans, who are probably hating this whole situation, but I guess their loss is our gain.

Sage Rosenfels
Vikings Quarterback
Being an Iowa guy, I certainly understand the rivalry between Minnesota and Wisconsin. So signing Brett has added a lot of fuel to that fire, so to speak. It should make for a fun season, that is for sure. As far as him coming in and being named as the starter, that is just the business of football. I am not bitter or anything else. Sure, I would love to be the starter, but I understand my role and will do whatever I can to help this football team win games. That is the bottom line. To be honest, I am excited about our chances this year, we have a really good football team. There is a lot of optimism around here, and a big part of that is because of No. 4. He is a Hall of Fame player and one of the game's all-time greats, so I am going to try to learn as much as I can from him, absolutely. I am always trying to take bits and pieces from every coach I have played for and every quarterback I have played alongside. That is what makes us better, more well-rounded players, and as a student of the game I am anxious to steal whatever knowledge I can from him. Another good thing that came out of Brett signing here, I suppose, was the fact that I am no longer an old guy! Heck, I am just a baby compared to that old man!

Visanthe Shiancoe
Vikings Tight End
Hell, yes, I am excited about Brett Favre coming to this football team. We had a great team before he got here, and he just made us even better.

Brett is a tremendous football player and he makes everyone on the field just that much better. As a savvy veteran, he has seen it all and done it all. For him, it is all about the little things. For instance, he doesn't give opposing defenses anything to key off of. He always looks off safeties. He can read and understand blitz packages and call audibles in a heartbeat. He is just always playing mind games and manipulating the defense, forcing them to stay honest. To see them get frustrated because they can't figure him out is awesome. It is amazing to watch him do his thing out there. Even with us receivers, he forces us to stay on our toes. We never know which one of us is going to get the ball. I mean, he may be looking at one receiver, and then he will turn and throw to another receiver in a split second. His peripheral vision is unbelievable. What he sees on the football field is extraordinary. For me, now, it is all about reps and about building that chemistry. Because once we have that, watch out!

> "Hell, yes, I am excited about Brett Favre coming to this football team. We had a great team before he got here, and he just made us even better."
> —Visanthe Shiancoe

Brad Childress
Vikings Head Coach

I am just glad that Brett is playing for us and not against us. I really am. You know, I say it all the time: you want to collect all the good football players that you can. There is no downside to that, whatsoever, at any position. That is how you win games in this league, with good football players. So, when the opportunity presented itself to get a guy like Brett Favre, we welcomed it. He makes our football team better. Not only that, he helps make every other player on this football team better. What I respect most about Brett is the fun and passion he genuinely has playing this game. While some players are very stoic, he is very emotional. He wears his heart on his sleeve. As a result, you always know where he is at—whether it is the highs or the lows.

The Packers' Brett Favre and Vikings head coach Brad Childress have a cordial discussion after the game on November 11, 2007, at Lambeau Field.

He certainly plays with a boyish enthusiasm for a guy who is going to be 40, that is for sure.

I am just glad that things have died down a little bit, it got pretty hectic there for a while. Everything leading up to this has been so … crazy, with the media and what have you. So I am glad that we are finally able to settle down and get to the business at hand. You know, everybody asks me about the now-infamous drive coming back from the airport to our practice facility, with the helicopter following

us. It is a little embarrassing that I got so busy talking to him that I actually missed my turn. It wasn't because I was so excited to finally realize that he was going to sign with us, either, it was because I have a big mouth. I was playing the role of tour guide. We were talking about the team, about our goals, about our expectations—all of that stuff. It was a good conversation, about football and about life. That was a big day, the day he signed, absolutely. I will say this, though, while I'm excited about our chances this year with Brett back there, I know that we have a lot of work to do and a long way to go. Nobody hands you anything in this league for free, you have to go out and earn it. It's time to go to work.

Antoine Winfield
Vikings Pro Bowl Cornerback
I'm very excited about having Brett on the team, absolutely. I have been playing against that guy for a long time. He is a great quarterback and is a lock for the Hall, so it is nice to have him with us as opposed to against us. He brings a lot to our locker room. He is a leader on and off the field. We trust and respect him because he has been there before and practically seen it all—from winning a Super Bowl to being named as the league MVP a few times. So he has a lot of credibility with the players, without a doubt. As a player, he is so competitive. He just wants to win at all costs every time he steps on the field. He brings so much energy, too, so much enthusiasm. He is always smiling and having fun, too, which is infectious for the other guys. He keeps us loose, that is for sure.

Bob Skoronski
Former Packers Tackle
I think someone who plays 17 years for a team and gives them the effort that Brett Favre gave to the Green Bay Packers has the right in the end to choose wherever he wants to play. So I don't have a problem with that. Look, the Packers decided that they didn't want Brett, as evidenced by the fact that he was not invited to training camp in

2008. I am not being critical of the organization, but to my understanding that was what transpired. I just think a guy who has put in that much time in the league has earned the right to finish his career the way he wants to, regardless of where that is.

I am not trying to say it was a good decision or a bad decision, but I don't have any problem with what he has done. Sure, Minnesota is a big rival, but players move from team to team all the time nowadays. It is a totally different era from when I

> *"He certainly plays with a boyish enthusiasm for a guy who is going to be 40, that is for sure."*
> —Brad Childress

played back in the '50s and '60s. So more power to him. Look, I don't think the Eagles were very happy when Reggie White left, either, but this is a business, and those things happen. Again, players should have every opportunity to play wherever they want to play.

As for why he is gone, who knows? Look, he probably got burnt out. I don't care who you are or what position you play, every player wants to retire at the end of the season but then they want to play again when the season starts up. That's the way it is in the NFL. This is a tough game, and it takes a toll on your body. How Brett has been able to play at such a high level, year-in and year-out for so long is just amazing. Say what you want to say, but Brett Favre served the Packers well. The guy played his heart out for this organization, and he gave us a lot of good years. I appreciate and respect that a great deal. He never missed a game, he rewrote the record books, and he brought us a Super Bowl. I think he has earned the right to go out on his own terms. Personally, I think Brett is a hell of a guy. I wish him well, I really do.

Now, am I happy about him choosing the Vikings? Of course not, but what the hell do I know about it? We would have all loved to have seen him retire as a Packer, but it just wasn't meant to be. Why that happened can be debated all you want, but the reality is that No. 4 is now playing for the Minnesota Vikings. It is time to move on, Brett certainly has.

Jim Taylor
Hall of Fame Packers Fullback
Brett still wants to compete and he still wants play, so he should be able to do so. If Minnesota feels like he can be productive, then good for Brett. I don't know why so many fans are so upset about it. I think a lot of them need to get a life and grow up. This is a business, and Brett wanted to continue playing football. That's what he does, he's a football player. That's his job. There are 32 teams in this league and just 32 starting-quarterback job openings. That's slim pickings, so I am sure he is thrilled to have a job doing what he loves to do. I know that there are some hard feelings, but it's Brett's choice as to where he wants to play, and he chose Minnesota. That was *his* choice, not the choice of Packer fans. So they need to get over it. I left Green Bay after nine seasons in 1967 to play for New Orleans, so I understand what it's like to go through that. For me, it was different in that I am from Louisiana and I was coming home. For Brett, he is going to the archrival. It doesn't matter, though. This is the entertainment business after all. Look, Brett is a competitor and he loves to compete. He's an outstanding player and a shoo-in for the Hall of Fame. He gave the Packers a lot of good years, so I wish him the best.

> *"If Minnesota feels like he can be productive, then good for Brett. I don't know why so many fans are so upset about it. I think a lot of them need to get a life and grow up."*
> —Jim Taylor

Bob Lurtsema
Former Vikings Defensive End and Founder of
Bob Lurtsema's Viking Update *Magazine*
Hell, yes, I am thrilled about getting Brett Favre in Minnesota. Kudos to [team owner] Zygi [Wilf] for getting this done, absolutely. Brett Favre is everything football stands for in my eyes: playing hurt,

attitude, love of the game, passion—you name it. He is the complete and total package. He's like a big kid out there, just playing football and having fun. He is an unbelievable competitor, too, maybe the best the game has ever known. He's fearless. He has never been afraid to throw into triple coverage, for better or for worse, and that is what makes him so unique. Sure, he has the all-time interceptions record, but I think that is more about him wanting to win at all costs as opposed to being selfish. He hates to lose and will do whatever it takes to rally his team to victory. A lot of quarterbacks would take a sack or throw the ball away if they thought they would throw an interception, or if they thought that they might get injured. Not Brett. That is

> *"He's fearless. He has never been afraid to throw into triple coverage, for better or for worse, and that is what makes him so unique."*
>
> —Bob Lurtsema

when the guy shines. He will step up into the pocket or scramble around until he can make something happen. He doesn't care about stats or records, he just wants to win. He's got that "all-in" attitude and doesn't give a shit about what the media will say about him if he messes up. That gunslinger mentality is the kind of football I love; the guy is a throwback.

A lot got made of him not going to training camp in Mankato, but I completely agree with the guy's decision not to come. It was a zoo down there this year, and for him to go through two weeks of autographs, interviews, questions, all the heckling from the disgruntled Packer fans, as well as the two-a-day practices—the guy would have been totally exhausted. Why put a veteran like that through all of that? It is not necessary. People need to understand that at 39 years old, your body changes. I retired at 36, and my body was way different at that point in my career than when it was when I was 26. So, in my opinion, him not being there was absolutely the right move. He is a very unique player, a superstar. No other player has 100 reporters

following him around all day the way Brett does. It's crazy. Are there different rules for Brett Favre? Does he receive special treatment? Absolutely. Do you know what, though? He's earned it. The players understand that. The fans and the media don't, but the people who matter do, and in the locker room that is all that matters.

As for the whole revenge thing, I am not sure what to make of it. I do know, however, that Packer GM Ted Thompson was the one who created this whole mess. From what I understand, it all started when Ted was on vacation and didn't want to call Brett back for whatever the reason. That was number one. Number two, don't ever, and I mean ever, ask an NFL veteran if he wants to retire on March 1. It *had* to be mandatory? Your body is still beat at that point, you still can't even think straight that early in the off-season. It takes at least six to eight weeks to recuperate after the season, to let your body recover from all the injuries and aches and pains. Well, for Brett, a 15-year vet, it probably takes even more time than that. So he dropped the ball in my eyes in forcing Brett's hand so early in the off-season for no apparent reason. Number three, Brett offered a good chunk of his own money to get Randy Moss on that roster. For whatever the reason, Ted wouldn't or couldn't pull the trigger to get it done. You see, Brett isn't about the money, he wants to win. Shit, he turned down $20 million from the Packers to come shake hands and sign autographs for goodness sakes. The guy doesn't need the cash, he needs Super Bowl rings. So, when he saw Moss go to New England, it was all over in my eyes. He wanted out. Believe me, there is no love lost between Brett Favre and Ted Thompson. The bottom line for this whole feud is this: I can't wait until November 1, when Brett runs out onto Lambeau Field wearing purple. What a story, you just can't make this stuff up.

> "Are there different rules for Brett Favre? Does he receive special treatment? Absolutely. Do you know what, though? He's earned it."
> —Bob Lurtsema

Rich Gannon
Former Pro Bowl Quarterback and Current NFL TV Analyst

I talked to Brett at length this summer, and he told me that he was torn with the decision of whether or not he wanted to come back at that time. He said that as a player 15, 20 years ago, he was just trying to find ways to make first downs and win games. He never worried too much about other people's perceptions in terms of what they thought of him. Now, all of a sudden, things are much different. He's had a Hall of Fame career and he *is* concerned about his legacy and about what the fans think of him. He said, "I am concerned, I am worried that people will misconstrue what my intentions are." So he struggled with that, absolutely. He confided in a number of current and former players, myself included, to kind of get their takes on coming back. At the end of the day, I think it boiled down to the fact that he still wants to play the game.

I have been through all of that and understand that completely. I can remember a number of times toward the end of my career where I would come home after a tough playoff loss or a season-ending injury and just say to myself, "I am done with this." Then April rolls around, and you start feeling a little bit better. Before you know it, you can't wait to get back out there and do it all over again. All veteran players go through that, it is just the nature of the game. Brett is no different. He wasn't sure if he still wanted to come back at first, but now he is committed. Beyond that, I think he looked at the situation in Minnesota and realized that it was a great fit for him. They have a great team, and he knows that system, which was a big factor in his ultimate decision. So I think it was a combination of both of those things that ultimately brought him back.

For me, the biggest adjustment with Brett going to Minnesota is going to be the dynamic between him and [head coach] Brad Childress. In talking to [former Vikings quarterback] Gus Frerotte, Brad is a very meticulous, hands-on type of a coach who has certain principles and guidelines that he wants to stick to. Well, Brett has never been in a situation like that. In Green Bay he was given the freedom to

I LOVE BRETT FAVRE

change plays and change protections at his discretion. He could hand-signal his receivers, he could throw the ball on the back side of a strong-side run—stuff like that can drive some coaches crazy. This is the last year of Brad's contract, so he is willing to roll the dice, I think. Look, the off-season training program is critical for a quarterback, especially a veteran coming to a new team. Just critical. To miss it altogether is a big gamble. But they think the reward outweighs the risk. So it will be interesting to see how that all shakes out this season.

As for the whole revenge aspect to this story, I know both sides of it from talking to a number of people within the Packer organization. Clearly, from the Packers' perspective, they never wanted him to retire. Even after he retired, there was talk of trying to convince him to come back. But at some point they decided that they had to move on. They couldn't be held hostage by the situation, they had to get ready for the draft and for the off-season. So they went with Aaron, which has worked out very well for them. Mike McCarthy is a big believer in guys being there for the off-season program, that is really important to him. He knows how vulnerable veteran players are to getting injuries and whatnot if they miss that time, and that kind of stuff can wreck your whole season if it gets out of control. So they decided not to roll the dice. For better or for worse, they went with Aaron and moved on. It was tough for them, though, no question. I don't think there is any animosity from the Packers' perspective, I really don't. From Brett's perspective, however, I am sure that there are some hard feelings. He says that there aren't, but it's just human nature to hold a grudge.

As far as what makes Brett Favre such a great player, a few things jump out at me. First of all, the most impressive record he has, without question, is his consecutive-starts record. For a quarterback to play the game the way he does, laying it all out on the line, that is absolutely phenomenal. People have no idea how significant that is. As a quarterback at this level, you get dinged up every single game, so for him to be able to keep doing what he is doing is just amazing. It speaks volumes about his toughness. He puts the team first and is all

about winning, regardless of the pain he may endure personally. You have to respect that. Plus, the players in the locker room totally feed off of that. I think that leadership by example makes everyone else try even harder. He plays the game like a kid. He is always smiling and laughing out there, doing crazy things. Teammates, coaches, fans, and even opponents really fell in love with that. That is the beauty of this game, the ability to just play it and enjoy it and put it all out there on Sundays— and that is what Brett does better than anybody. So, whether you are a Packer fan or a Viking fan, you just have to tip your hat to the guy.

> *"He is always smiling and laughing out there, doing crazy things.... That is the beauty of this game, the ability to just play it and enjoy it and put it all out there on Sundays—and that is what Brett does better than anybody."*
>
> —Rich Gannon

As for Brett the person, he is a great guy. Not only do I have a ton of respect for him as a player, I really admire what he has done from a community service aspect. He has been a great role model for kids and he has a great heart as far as giving back to various causes. It is so hard not to like a guy like Brett. Sure, he is controversial and, sure, he is guilty of flip-flopping as far as retirement and holding the Vikings hostage and all of that goes, but at the end of the day he is one of the greatest players the NFL has ever seen. That bottom line is this: would you want Brett Favre on your team? Most coaches would say yes, maybe not publicly, but the reality is he would make most teams in this league better the second he stepped on to the field.

With regards to how his reception will be up in Green Bay when he takes the field as a Viking, it is not going to be very warm—that much I can promise you. It's not going to be pretty. I have spent a lot of time up there doing preseason games [on TV], and the fans are upset about him choosing to go to Minnesota. Brett was their guy, he was *their* quarterback for a lot of years. So going to New York was one

thing, but going across the state line to Minnesota was quite another in their eyes. One thing is for sure, it's going to be a hell of a season.

Jim Marshall
Former Pro Bowl Vikings Defensive End and Previous Record Holder for Consecutive Games Played
As for him signing with Minnesota, hey, if it helps them win the Super Bowl, then I think it would be fantastic. I'm just very happy for Brett and I'm very happy for the team. As for the streak [270 consecutive games and 20 consecutive seasons without missing a game], I would be honored to have Brett break it. I would absolutely love it. If anybody should have it, it should be him. He deserves it. He is so tough and plays the game with such passion, I just have a lot of respect for him. He is a great, great player—definitely one of the best ever to play this game.

Mike Morris
Former Vikings Center and Current Twin Cities Sports Talk Radio Host
This all works great for me. Brett Favre is the kind of guy who I wished was on my team when I was playing all those years. He is one hell of a football player, that is for sure. He is just an amazing competitor and he is all about winning. What else can you say? The guy is a winner. And he is so tough and durable, his consecutive-starts numbers as a quarterback are crazy. I can't imagine that will ever be broken. Ever. As a Vikings fan, let's just hope he can do for us what he did in Green Bay. I think the fans were so eager to jump on his bandwagon here because they are so desperate for a Super Bowl. Everyone keeps saying, "We are just one piece away," and all of that, and he looks to be that "piece." So let's just hope it all works out. He has struggled mightily in the Dome, though, I will say that. For whatever the reason he has not played well in there. Hopefully, that will all change, though.

As for the whole revenge thing, I think it is just what Brett said— if you're here just for those two games against Green Bay, then you are in for a rude awakening. I think he's in it for the long haul, I really

do. The only way to really get back at the Packer organization is to prove that you're good enough to lead another team to a Super Bowl. That is the big get-back in my eyes. I am sure he wants to get back at certain people over there, but in reality things have changed. That is not the same team he played for. It's not the same management that he signed with; the coach is gone, and all of his old teammates are gone. The only guy that is still there, I guess, is Ted Thompson, and that is probably who the beef is with. The team moved on, and in the end he was the odd man out. The only problem for Brett is that he has blown up the her- itage, because while everything else has changed—the fans are still the same. That sucks for him, but he's getting $25 million out of the deal, so I think he'll get over it.

> *"I used to room with Jim McMahon...who won a Super Bowl with the Bears and then went on to play for the Packers and Vikings—yet nobody had a problem with that."*
> *—Mike Morris*

The reality is that players move around. I played for sev- eral teams over my career, and that is just the way it is. We have a short life-span in this league as players, and we all want to play until they tell us we can't. It's all we know, and none of us want to hang it up. So I have no problem whatsoever with Brett continuing to play. Hell, I am happy for the guy. Hey, I used to room with Jim McMahon, and there was a guy, a quarterback nonetheless, who won a Super Bowl with the Bears and then went on to play for the Packers and Vikings—yet nobody had a problem with that. The fans in Chicago still embrace him as their own. That's how fans are. So the Green Bay fans will get over No. 4 wearing purple eventually.

Darrell Thompson
Former Packers Running Back
I played with Brett for three seasons early on in his career, his forma- tive years, but even then you could tell that he was going to be pretty

special. He made everybody around him better. His passion for the game and his willingness to sacrifice his body for the good of the team was infectious. The guy just led by example, no doubt about it. Whether it was running wind sprints or playing hurt, he was out there leading the way. The guy is just a competitor. He is also a great guy and a great teammate—just completely down to earth. He's funny and he's laid back. That is the Brett Favre I know.

My mom was born and raised in Mississippi, and I have a ton of family down there, so Brett and I got along right out of the gates. We spent time together in the locker room, the weight room, and at the bars in Green Bay. We would hang out and talk about whatever, it was fun. He used to love to tell me stories about what life was like down in his hometown of Kiln. I remember him telling me that the town was so small that one of his buddies who farmed used to drive an old tractor in the nude. That way he wouldn't get his clothes all dirty, and when he was finished, his dad would just hose him off. Crazy stuff like that.

> "He used to love to tell me stories about what life was like down in his hometown of Kiln.... One of his buddies...used to drive an old tractor in the nude. That way he wouldn't get his clothes all dirty."
> —Darrell Thompson

As for the secrets of his success, I think it all goes back to preparation. He studies hard, does a lot of film work, and is really a student of the game. A lot of people just think he is a river boat gambler, but in reality he prepares very diligently before every game. He does a lot more homework than I think people give him credit for. Don't let that aw-shucks southern drawl fool you, he's a really smart guy. Beyond that, the guy is a really hard worker who puts in the time. A lot of people might not see it that way, but trust me, he works his tail off.

One of his best traits is his ability to switch between Brett the funny jokester in the locker room and Brett the intense quarterback

in the huddle. He can turn it on and off in a heartbeat. I mean, one second during a timeout or something he would be talking about drinking a beer after the game or about a cute girl up in the stands, and the next he would be completely focused on calling the play. It was amazing. It was like a light switch, I have never seen anything like it before. The bottom line with Brett was that he loved to have fun. He kept it light, and as a result I think we all fed off of that. He would set the tone for all of us, and that is what made him such a good leader.

Stu Voigt
Former Vikings Tight End and Current Vikings Radio Analyst
I am kind of caught in the middle of this whole fiasco in that I am from Wisconsin but played my whole career with the Vikings. So I have a unique perspective about the whole thing, that is for sure. Growing up in Wisconsin, I was a big Packer fan, and other than Vince [Lombardi], there aren't too many bigger Packers than Brett Favre. He is an icon in Wisconsin, so for him to come to the enemy is a pretty big deal over there. Packer fans just assumed that he would retire as a Packer and that would be it, and now they are in a state of denial. I just think he has earned the right to write the ending to his own story. That's my take on the whole situation....

Brett obviously had a falling out with Ted Thompson and the folks over there [in Green Bay] in the front office, but nobody ever really saw this coming—where he would be playing for the Vikings. That really opened a wound for a lot of people. For a lot of fans that now makes him Enemy No. 1, the ultimate traitor who can never be forgiven. Wisconsin fans are extremely loyal, and his coming to Minnesota has really tarnished his image in a lot of eyes over there. That is sad because he gave the Packers a lot of good years. Hey, this is a tremendous rivalry we have up here. The fans want blood and guts, that is how these two feel about each other.

I think that Brett came here because he genuinely thinks he can win a world championship with this team. I am sure this was the only place he even considered, where all the "pieces were in place," so to

speak. He knows the West Coast [offense] system and he knows the coaching staff, so it was a great fit for him. Plus, Minnesota has a great team, which is a huge factor. All he has to do is hand it to Adrian Peterson 25 times a game, and in many instances that will be enough to win. The future is now for Brett Favre, and this team is ready to go. The only thing that they were really missing was a quarterback. ...

> "Packer fans just assumed that he would retire as a Packer and that would be it, and now they are in a state of denial. I just think he has earned the right to write the ending to his own story."
> — Stu Voigt

He knows how to lead a team of men to a championship. That is a big deal. He knows how to get guys to buy into his style of play, and from there he just leads the way. He wants the ball in big games, too, which is also a sign of a great competitor. Not everybody relishes that role, but he does. There is a downside to that, too, with his whole gunslinger mentality of forcing balls sometimes. But that is Brett Favre, you live with him and you die with him. Who else do you want to give the ball to when you are down by a field goal with two minutes to go? The bottom line, though, is that the guy is just an amazing football player. He is one of the greatest quarterbacks of all time, no question.

Dick Hantak
Longtime NFL Referee

As a referee, my basic responsibility was to protect the quarterback. We don't watch downfield, we keep our eyes on him to make sure he is not taken advantage of. As a result, we get to know those guys a little better than the other players. Well, I had worked quite a few Green Bay games ... and I had gotten to know Brett a little bit over the years. The last game I worked was up in New York, and Brett was still playing with Green Bay. It was late in the game, and he was on the sideline because the Jets were way ahead. We went to a TV timeout, and

during those brief few moments I went over to speak with him. I told him that I was retiring and that I just wanted to tell him how much I had enjoyed working behind him for all those years. So I reached out to shake his hand, and instead of shaking it, he pulled me in and gave me a hug. It was totally unexpected, but it was a moment I will never forget.

Favre hugs retiring referee Dick Hantak on the sideline in the fourth quarter of a road loss to the Jets in December 2002. *Photo courtesy of Getty Images*

As far as our professional relationship, Brett was easy to get along with. He never complained and he was always very respectful of us [the officials] out there. I appreciated that a great deal. A lot of quarterbacks liked to scream and holler when calls didn't go their way, but Brett never did that kind of stuff. … He has a real passion to play this game and is just very enthusiastic about what he does. In fact, sometimes that passion got him into trouble—as evidenced by the fact that the "Brett Rule" was infamously named in his honor. The rule refers to players no longer being allowed to take off their helmets on the field of play and results in a 15-yard personal foul penalty. It was because of him that the rule was put into place. He would take off his helmet after throwing a touchdown pass and hold it up in the air while he was racing down the field to celebrate with his teammates. Well, the other players started doing it, and eventually the league decided to put an end to it. So, however his legacy is written, that will undoubtedly be a part of it, as well.

> "My take on it is that he wanted to leave Green Bay more than they wanted him to leave Green Bay. The way it all went down wasn't very pretty."
> —Jerome Bettis

Chuck Foreman
Former Pro Bowl Vikings Running Back

As far as Brett coming to Minnesota, all I can say is that there is no loyalty in football. None. The only reason we all played with the Vikings for so many years was because we couldn't go anywhere else. There was no free agency in my day. Most of us would have left for more money, without a doubt—as long as the Vikings didn't offer to match it. That was then and this is now, though, and times have certainly changed. So, to see Brett Favre coming to Minnesota, I say more power to him. It has to be nice to come here on your own terms and still get $25 million to boot. Man, times have changed. I am sure the Packer fans are upset, but they will get over it. Players come and

go, that is how it is in pro sports today. I am just glad that he came here instead of somewhere else. He is a great quarterback and he will definitely help this team. He gives us our best shot at getting back to the Super Bowl in a long time, so I am really excited about it.

Jerome Bettis
Former Pro Bowl Steelers Running Back and Current
Sunday Night Football *Analyst*

Why did Brett Favre come back with Minnesota? That is the million-dollar question. The opinions and theories are out there, for sure. For me, I think he just wants to play. Because he won a Super Bowl early in his career, I don't think that is the big driving force in his decision to come back with Minnesota. I just think he loves the game and wants to keep playing [until] they tell him he can't anymore. I really do. I think that there is a revenge factor, though, no question. My take on it is that he wanted to leave Green Bay more than they wanted him to leave Green Bay. The way it all went down wasn't very pretty, so I think he wants to have the last say in the matter. That's just my opinion on it. The guy is a throwback, he really is. It's not about the money for him, it's about playing and having fun. And although his actions may seem otherwise, he's not a prima donna. He's an everyday guy, and that is what his teammates really appreciate and respect about him. Hey, who knows? Maybe he will lead that team to the Super Bowl. It could happen—they are really good. One thing is for sure, it is going to be a treat to see him play up in Green Bay on November 1, that is for sure. We are all very excited about that. That is the game everybody wants to see. The fans are going to be pumped up; it is going to be scary.

Paul Hornung
Packers Hall of Fame Halfback

Brett wearing purple? Hell, that's all right by me. He can still play at a high level, and I wish him nothing but the best. I remember about five years ago when the two of us were having dinner one night. He had asked me about retiring. Well, I just told him that he should play as

long as he could. I said "Play until they tell you that you can't play anymore. Play as long as you absolutely can, hell, yes. Because you're not going to have any more fun than what you are having right now. Once you quit and you are retired, you will have a good life, but it's not going to be as good as when you're playing." So that was my advice to Brett.

I know Packer fans are upset, absolutely. I understand that, but they'll get past it. Sure, he'll get booed when he comes back to Lambeau, but he doesn't care. He's tough. Plus, he's making $12 million, so he'll be all right! Look, years from now, when this has all blown over and he's retired for good, they'll welcome him back. In my opinion, he's the greatest player in the history of that entire organization. So he's earned the right to do whatever he wants to do, as far as I'm concerned. The guy just wants to play, that's it. Nothing more, nothing less. I did the color [analysis] for Vikings TV games for five seasons, so I know all about this rivalry from both sides. It's all in good fun. That's what makes football so interesting. Just for the hell of it, I even put on a No. 4 Favre Vikings jersey and took a picture of myself in it and mailed it to Brett. I signed it, "Hey, Brett, you never looked so good!"

Personally, I think Brett is a great kid. He has been nice enough to come down here to Louisville [Kentucky] to be on my television show on a couple of occasions, and I really appreciated that. I remember one time, years ago, we went out golfing at Valhalla. Anyway, he had a handful of bloody marys on the front nine and then it started to get really hot out, so I sent our caddie back to get us a couple dozen cold beers. It was a great day. Then, after golf we went back to do my TV show. It was a full house, and people were excited to see him. Now, this was around the time when his drinking was getting a little out of control and he had some public problems with painkillers, and the [NFL] commissioner had even told him that he had to start taking it easy. He had been chastised publicly in the papers, and it was a big deal. So, during the interview, I asked him about it. Brett sits up, looks me straight in the eye and says, "You know, Paul, I haven't had a drink in nine months." I nearly laughed my ass off right then and there, but I just kept a straight face.

The Media Love Brett Favre

Don Banks
Sports Illustrated
Having covered the Vikings for four years in the late '90s, and now having lived in Wisconsin through at least part of an NFL season, I still can't quite wrap my mind around the image of Favre wearing a helmet with those familiar horns on it. I suppose we'll all get used to it pretty quickly, the way the Jets' green and white looked somewhat normal on Favre by season's end, but at the moment it still seems a completely foreign visual. Like Derek Jeter in Red Sox colors, getting a bear hug from Big Papi.

Seth Wickersham
ESPN
You'll find plenty of folks, many in the media—many who should know better—who will rip Favre for being exactly what we've always loved about our athletes: human. Imperfect. Flawed. Daring. Honest. Yes, he changes his mind a lot. So often, in fact, that it's laughable....

Talk all you want about how he's ruining his legacy, but as he says, "It's mine." And so it's fitting that Favre prepped for this comeback

> *"You'll find plenty of folks, many in the media—many who should know better—who will rip Favre for being exactly what we've always loved about our athletes: human."*
> —Seth Wickersham

on a high school field, surrounded by kids whose football careers will also end earlier than they wish. He's one of them, really. He always will wish his career lasted longer. Quarterbacks often say they only have so many throws in their arms, and those throws do you no good once you're retired. Favre literally wants to throw until he can't. It's noble. "I'm in it for the right reasons," he said. "If people can't understand that, I'm sorry." No need to apologize.

Dawn Mitchell
Twin Cities TV Sports Anchor and Fox Sports NFL Analyst
I have covered Brett for most of my career: two years on a daily basis in Green Bay, another five indirectly in Chicago, and now six in Minnesota with the Vikings. So I've had a pretty unique perspective on his career from a lot of different vantage points. With regards to him choosing to come to Minnesota to play for the Vikings, it is an absolutely huge story. Huge. This is a really big rivalry, no question. Maybe the biggest in the NFL. I remember covering the Packers up in Green Bay my first year and just being blown away when I saw how nervous they were to face the Vikings in the Metrodome. To prepare for it they actually pumped in super-loud crowd noise into the Don Hutson [practice] Center, so the players could get used to it. You literally had to hold your hands over your ears, it was so loud in there. Those games are always a battle, and the fans live for them.

As for Brett the person, he is really a nice guy. He is such a polarizing figure, though, because he speaks his mind and he wears his heart out on his sleeve. And if you don't agree with him, he doesn't care. Brett is the kind of person who puts it all out on the line. As a result, people either love him or hate him. They either think he is the

greatest guy in the world or they think he is a prima donna. There is no gray area with him. I guess when people are just true to themselves and put it all out there, there is really no in-between—and that is Brett Favre to a tee. He is very funny, too. Being around him in the locker room or in the press room, he was a lot of fun. In Green Bay he was always razzing Frank Winters, or "Franky Bag-a-donuts," as he called him, or Mark Chmura, or whomever. He was always trying to pull practical jokes and just having fun. That is the side of Brett Favre no one really gets to see. He is not the kind of guy who forgets you in the off-season, either. One time I was covering a Milwaukee Brewers game, and he came over and said, "Hey, Dawn, how are you doing?" We started talking, and I told him that I had recently gone to his steak-house up in Green Bay. So we start talking about what I ate and about what things I think he should have on the menu. It was crazy. He is a very real person, though, very laid back, very down to earth, and obviously very misunderstood.

As for Brett the player, what can you say? The guy is a Hall of Famer. He is so tough. Almost to his own detriment, he will play through an injury. Durability is a big thing with him.... He is the game's greatest of all time in that regard. As tough as he is physically, though, he is even tougher mentally. Most quarterbacks get frazzled when they throw interceptions or get sacked. Not Brett. He shakes it off and comes back even harder. It is like a good goalie in the NHL who can stay focused after letting in a big goal. That is Brett. And who runs the two-minute drill better than Brett Favre? How many last-second drives have we seen him orchestrate over the years? He loves that stuff. Beyond that, he is a risk taker. He is just willing to do whatever it takes to win.

With regards to the whole revenge angle to this story, I think there is a lot more to this than people think. I think it all started with Brett wanting Ted Thompson to sign Randy Moss a few years ago. I have it on good sources that Brett put a million dollars of his own money on the table to try to get Moss signed and make it work with the salary cap. He wanted to get him on board because Brett is all about winning.

They had a great team that year, and Brett figured Randy would be the missing piece. So, when Ted didn't pull the trigger on getting him, and he wound up going to New England instead for a fourth-round draft pick, Brett got really upset. Again, Brett is the kind of person who wears his heart on his sleeve. He speaks his mind—whether rightly or wrongly, smartly or businesswise—and that cause a big rift. Then it was not handled very well when Ted traded Brett. Reportedly, he let him know in a text message, of all things, and even threw in a few choice, colorful words along with it. I think that Mike McCarthy just got stuck in the middle of it all, to tell you the truth.

Having said all of that, knowing Brett, I don't think he went to the Vikings for revenge. The reality is that the Vikings have a kick-butt defense; they have the best running back in the game in Adrian Peterson; they have Bernard Berrian and Percy Harvin at receiver; and maybe most important, the team's offensive coordinator is Darrell Bevell, one of his best friends, and he runs an offense that Brett can call in his sleep. Plus, he knows that he won't have to throw the ball a million times a game like he had to do in New York. Here he can hand it off to Peterson and not be expected to do it all. That is very appealing to him. So I think all of those things went into his decision to come here. The revenge? That is just the cherry on top, in my eyes. Now, are Packer fans hurt? Obviously. I would be, too. But again, I don't think he came here to hurt them. I think he came here to win a Super Bowl on a very good veteran team that most analysts agree is "a quarterback away from winning it all.". . .

I got to know Brett's family a little bit during my time in Green Bay, and they have been very good to me over the years. They have always been straight with me and they have never lied to me, which I really respect a great deal. I will say this, though, from talking to certain members of his family, there was never any doubt that Brett wanted to come back. . . . I remember getting one particular text about a week before the news broke of him deciding to sign. It was shortly after Tarvaris Jackson had gone down with a knee injury, and the text basically asked me what I thought about the current quarterback

situation. "How are the quarterbacks looking?" That was it. Now, that was not the style of text that I had ever received from any of his family, so I started to figure Brett was using his family to ask me some questions. His family knew that I would be honest with them and they trusted my opinion. We communicated back and forth from there, and I was able to be a go-between for them, to get information.... I knew after that, it was only a matter of time before he signed, and sure enough, that next week it all went down. I got a text the night before he signed that read, "I think he is going to do it."...

I will never forget the game back in 2007 when he broke the NFL's long-standing all-time touchdown record, which was previously held by Dan Marino. The Packers were in Minnesota playing the Vikings at the Dome, and I was working as a sideline reporter for Fox Sports. It was a nationally televised game, and the network wanted the exclusive after the game, to talk to him. Well, Brett was so focused on winning the game that he wouldn't commit to doing an interview. All the producers are just freaking out at this point because they don't have a commitment from him that he will talk to us. Meanwhile, I have been talking to their PR guy and working every angle. I finally told him at halftime to please relay a message to Brett that "Dawn wants to do an interview." He returned the message back to me by saying that he was favorable to it if they win. Finally, late in the fourth quarter, he already has the record—he threw No. 421 to Greg Jennings—I go back over to their PR guy to see

> "Who runs the two-minute drill better than Brett Favre? How many last-second drives have we seen him orchestrate over the years? He loves that stuff."
> —Dawn Mitchell

what's up. He looks at me and says, "First Deanna [his wife], then Dawn." I was like, "Yes!" The network people were so excited that I was able to pull it off, otherwise they would have been totally screwed.

Sure enough, they wound up winning the game 23–16, and afterward he went over and hugged his wife. Immediately after that he

Brett Favre lifts wide receiver Greg Jennings up onto his shoulders after Jennings caught the record-breaking 421st touchdown pass of Favre's career against the Vikings on September 30, 2007, in the Metrodome.

looked for me and then started walking over to do the interview. Now, because of time constraints, I only have time for one question. My producer is screaming at me, telling me that under no uncertain terms do they want Brett to say, "The record means nothing to me," which they felt would be really disrespectful to a lot of people. They knew

that if I worded this question the wrong way that he would either give me a one-word answer, or tell me that he didn't care about the record. Either way I would be hosed, so I was pretty nervous. I just calmly told them that I knew Brett and that I knew exactly what to ask him. At this point they are just freaking out. Pam Oliver was their normal sideline reporter, but I was filling in for her, so they didn't know much about me. Finally, Brett comes over, and I say, "He is your new touchdown pass king, but Brett Favre is more concerned with victories. Brett, you got both today, you are 4–0 this season *and* you have the touchdown record, how does this compare for you in your career?" It was awesome. He got really emotional and just started talking about what a great feeling it was and about how the team had overcome so much adversity to get to that point. It was hands down one of the greatest moments of my career, just amazing. Needless to say, my producers were thrilled.

So everyone thinks that Brett is an egomaniac who is all about the glory and about hogging the limelight, but in reality it couldn't be further from the truth. Winning is the first thing for Brett, not being on TV or setting records. Luckily for me, I knew the difference. The way I see it, the bottom line for Brett is that he wants to go out as a winner. If he can go out with a Super Bowl victory, that is his perfect ending. That is what it is all about for him. I don't think he cares about his legacy the way everyone else cares about it. He just wants to win. Look, I don't begrudge any athlete that can't give up playing and doing what he loves, whether that is Michael Jordan or Roger Clemens or Brett Favre. If he's having fun and he thinks he can contribute and win, then more power to him. I wish him all the success in the world.

Steve Sabol
President, NFL Films

How do I feel about him coming back? Shit, I love it! This is all a part of the mythology of Brett Favre. He is such a fascinating person. His story is so unique. Football has been Brett's whole life, and he doesn't

want to let it go. He still loves to play. He still has the fire, the desire, and the competitive spirit. He still gets that rush, that adrenaline on Sundays, and that is what he is addicted to. Brett is good for the game, so I am thrilled he came back. The fact that he came back to his former rival just makes the story even that much more interesting. Look, every great athlete likes to have that "I told you so" moment to prove their naysayers wrong, and this may just be Brett's moment. You just can't count him out, no way. He is one of the greatest competitors in the history of this game.

Like any mythological hero, Brett is often undone by the very gifts that make him heroic—and that is his willingness to take risks. That is the quality that made Arnold Palmer beloved to this day. Even though Jack Nicklaus was a better golfer, people loved Arnold because he would always go for the birdies no matter what and take risks. Sure, sometimes he would end up in the sand or in the trees, but the fans loved him for trying. I think that is what everybody loves about Brett, that bravado, that confidence that his gamble will ultimately pay off. He is just not afraid to fail. Beyond that, Brett is the kind of player who can elevate the play of his teammates. He makes everybody around him better. He is also just a regular guy, a guy you would love to have a beer with. In my eyes, that unique combination of things is what makes him so appealing.

> "There is never going to be another Brett Favre in the future. So I think all football fans, whether they are in Minnesota, Green Bay, or anywhere should be lucky that we can enjoy him do what he does best on Sundays."
> —Steve Sabol

What people don't know about Brett is that he is actually a pretty funny guy. I remember being down in "the Kiln" [Mississippi] one time with him and his dad, Big Irv, his mom, Bonita, and his grandmother. We were sitting around talking, and I made a comment about

how hot it was. Brett chimes in and says, "It's hotter here than two rats fuckin' in a wool sock!" I just about fell off my chair. We have miked him several times for NFL Films, too, and he always says some really funny stuff. I remember one time we had him miked up for a game at Lambeau, and the ball was wet, so he says, "This thing is slicker than owl shit!" He just has that charming, aw-shucks way of putting things.

Here is the thing to remember in all of this, there is never going to be another Brett Favre in the future. So I think all football fans, whether they are in Minnesota, Green Bay, or anywhere should be lucky that we can enjoy him do what he does best on Sundays. I don't know when it will eventually come to an end, but until then I am going to watch and enjoy. He is truly a one-of-a-kind player. Where guys like Peyton Manning and Tom Brady are admired, Brett Favre is cherished. There is a big difference.

Brett has that sort of mongrel constitution in his body where he can take so much punishment. When I think of all the records he holds, the one that will be unchallengeable and never broken is the consecutive-starts streak for a quarterback. I mean, for a quarterback to start 270 straight games, that is just unbelievable. It wouldn't be fair to call him the last of his kind because the game has never seen anyone remotely like him. Because of his daring style, which endeared him to so many fans, he made more good plays and more bad plays than any quarterback in history. I have never seen anyone throw so many good passes from so many different positions. We could put together a highlight reel of him throwing completions from his back, on his knees, falling forward, falling backward, flipping it underhand, or what have you. It is remarkable. Marlon Brando once said about acting, "You are only as good as you dare to be bad." Well, to me, Brett Favre always dared to be bad. That is what makes him so good.

Kevin Seifert
ESPN Football Analyst

Favre's decision to move from Green Bay to Minnesota is historic. For him to come here was so random. I mean, there was nothing in terms

of his life and career that connected him to Minnesota. It wasn't like he grew up here and always wanted to finish his career here, or that he was a lifelong Vikings fan and had dreamt of playing here. So he clearly wanted to be here for his own reasons. What those real reasons are, whether it is about winning a Super Bowl or about getting revenge against his old team, remains the big question.

This is a very heated rivalry, Minnesota and Green Bay. You don't see the passions of a rivalry inflamed too often like this. With free agency and so much player movement in this generation of players, a lot of rivalries seem to have been lost. Not this one, Favre has rekindled it in a big way. There are really a lot of people who care deeply about the whole thing, and that has all come out since he signed. The culmination of all of this will come to a head on November 1 up in Green Bay, when he steps onto Lambeau Field. What a sight that is going to be. It is going to be historic in the annals of not only both teams, but of the NFL. Never has there been anything like this before, where a guy of his caliber goes from one division rival to another. Never. Without trying to exaggerate, I really think it is going to be one of the most dramatic moments in NFL history.

As for Favre the player, he can still compete at a very high level. No question. Favre is just one of those rare players who can seemingly always figure out how to win a game. That to me is the number-one thing that the Vikings are going to be gaining out of this: a player who is well versed in those little veteran tricks and nuances that can oftentimes mean the difference between winning and losing.

Eric Nelson
Twin Cities Sports Talk Radio Host
Brett Favre is beyond polarizing, he is a human lightning rod. To go from being an icon to a pariah, almost overnight, is amazing. When he takes the field in Lambeau on November 1, I think that is going to be one of the more surreal settings we have ever seen. You can't make this stuff up. It's crazy, just over the top. I mean, if you were to take a poll right now in Wisconsin, he would probably rank behind warm beer,

moldy cheese, and cold brats. He is Public Enemy No. 1 over there. No doubt about it. How amped up is he going to be when he runs out of the tunnel that game? It will be insane. It will be really emotional for the Packer players, too, especially the defensive players who had to put up with him for all those years. He won't be wearing a red [practice] jersey, either, he's no longer untouchable, so I am sure they are going to try to get to him early and often. I wouldn't be surprised if there

> *"The culmination of all of this will come to a head on November 1 up in Green Bay, when he steps onto Lambeau Field. What a sight that is going to be."*
> —*Kevin Seifert*

was some sort of bounty put out on him, unofficially of course, to see who gets the first sack or what have you. It is going to be quite a sight.

There used to be a universal love for Brett Favre, with maybe the exceptions being in Minnesota and Chicago, but not anymore. And even Vikings and Bears fans respected him as a player. They may have hated him, but they acknowledged that he was one of the all-time greats. Now, however, because of his flip-flopping and choosing to play for the enemy, that has all changed. His legacy is tarnished in most people's eyes. A lot of people still love him, but there are many, many more who are just plain sick and tired of his act.

I have heard people say, "Well, Vince Lombardi left Green Bay, too." Yes, he did, but he didn't go to their archrival, he went to Washington. The only thing you could compare it to today would be Derek Jeter going to the Red Sox, and that wouldn't even be close to how big a deal this is between Minnesota and Wisconsin, in my eyes. This is without a doubt the NFL's top geographical rivalry. No question. Two neighboring states with people who absolutely hate each other, it makes for an awesome border battle. The addition of Brett just adds fuel to this inferno. Minnesota fans are so damn desperate for a Super Bowl, though, they really don't care who they sign at this point. They just want to win.

As for the rift between Brett and Ted Thompson, there is more
than meets the eye with this. It has become like the Brad Pitt–Jennifer
Aniston situation, really ugly. I am sure this is just a part of why Brett
came back, though. I think that the bottom line for him is that he loves
to play. Check that—he loves to play on Sundays. He hates all of the
other BS—the practices, meetings, training camp, and what have
you—that comes along with it, but he loves to play and he still feels
that he can compete at a high level....

The [media] coverage has just been so over the top, from the helicopter footage of him signing to the day-to-day Brett sightings, it has
been crazy. So many rumors and so much disinformation, you literally couldn't keep up with it all. People were constantly asking me,
"What's going to happen with Favre?" You couldn't escape it. Then,
when he announced that he wasn't going to sign after all, just before
training camp, that was like somebody had taken all the air out of a
hot air balloon. You could feel it in the air down in Mankato [train-
ing camp], where it was like a wake. When he finally did sign a few
weeks later, it was as if we had won the war. Just amazing stuff. Of
course, the whole thing was orchestrated, obviously. He just didn't
want to go to camp, yet they felt like they had to go through this whole
saga. The tail was wagging the dog, and if there is one thing we know
about Brett is that he plays by his own set of rules. The bottom line is
that he garners interest. Whether you love him or hate him, everybody
has an opinion. He is just the ultimate water-cooler topic.

Dark Star
Longtime Twin Cities Sports Talk Radio Host
Athletes leave all the time, that is nothing new. But I have never really
seen anything quite like this in all my years, to tell you the truth. I have
seen a bunch, too. I remember living in Los Angeles when Joe
Namath went to the Rams, and it was a pretty big deal. It was horri-
fying, though. I don't ever think he took his cape off. He was just a
shell of his former self and really sad to see. It was the same deal when
Johnny Unitas went to San Diego, really a sad deal. For me, as a native

Ohioan, the worst was seeing Frank Robinson leave Cincinnati and go to Baltimore. It was like a black cloud hung over the state for about two years, just unbelievable. So I understand what the folks in Wisconsin are going through. Seeing your heroes move on is tough, no question. It is even tougher when they choose to go to your number-one archrival, which is what happened in this situation. And that is why this is such a big deal. I mean, who in their wildest dreams would have ever imagined Brett Favre wear-

> *"Minnesota fans went from hating this guy to loving him in about 10 minutes.*
> *It was the craziest damn thing I have ever seen."*
> *—Dark Star*

ing purple? Nobody. It's insane. It's almost like pro wrestling, where the villain becomes the hero and vice versa.

In my eyes, aside from the Twins winning the World Series, this is the biggest sports story in this town over the last 25 years. It is so intoxicating because the tentacles reach out so far. The fans have gone completely nuts for this guy—it is remarkable. Doing my radio show, I see it firsthand every day. If I throw a question out there about Favre, like, "Is he good for the Vikings?"—I could go four straight hours with every phone line in the studio lit up nonstop. Everybody wants to weigh in on this thing, they've all got an opinion. I have never seen a player cause this kind of fervor, never. Minnesota fans went from hating this guy to loving him in about 10 minutes. It was the craziest damn thing I have ever seen.

That game in Lambeau on November 1 will be *the* most significant regular-season game in franchise history. No question about it. When he takes that first step onto the frozen tundra, a thousand hearts are going to break. It is going to be quite the scene, it really is. A lot of Packer fans are thoroughly disgusted, and I don't blame them. I would be pissed, too. Most will say it never should have come to this and that this just never should have happened. Ted Thompson is really under the gun over there. He is the bad guy in their eyes, not Brett. I would

have to believe that guy's job has got to be on the line for this thing, especially if the Vikings win that game in dramatic fashion and go deep into the playoffs. The way I see it, he drove the nails through the hands of the greatest quarterback in Green Bay history.

It will be interesting to see how this all plays out, that is for sure. Because anything less than a serious run at the Super Bowl is going to be deemed as a failure by most fans around here. It's a singular variable, Super Bowl or bust. That's it. Because if Favre gets injured or this team fails to make it to the playoffs, people are going to be really upset, and there are going to be some folks getting canned, I guarantee it. And then what? He comes back next year as a 41-year-old quarterback with a torn rotator cuff? The future is right now, and it's now or never for the Vikings.

Sid Hartman
Longtime Twin Cities Sports Columnist for Star Tribune *and Radio Host*
I think Brett realized that this was probably his last opportunity to get to a Super Bowl, so he took it. This is a pretty good football team with a great running back, and he knows that. I think that his buddy, Darrell Bevell, had a lot to do with him coming here, too. Their friendship combined with the fact that they run a similar West Coast offense here were the other big factors in him coming. Brett knows this system and is comfortable in it. He is a hell of a player, and I am excited to see what he can do.

That game up in Lambeau, though, that is going to be something else. To see him return to Green Bay wearing a Vikings uniform is going to be quite a sight. And it will only enhance what most feel is the best rivalry in the NFL. A lot of people don't realize this, but we used to root for the Packers in this town way back when. That's right. You see, before we had pro football here [prior to 1961], we used to listen to all the Packer games on the radio. The fans got acclimated to them, and they became like our hometown team. Ray Scott was their longtime announcer, and those games were a big deal—especially when they would play Chicago. Fans would travel to Green Bay to

watch them in those days, too, much like fans from Iowa and the Dakotas come to Minneapolis to watch the Vikings today. Things have changed over the years, but make no mistake about it, this is the best rivalry in football. No question.

Paul Allen
Twin Cities Sports Talk Radio Host and Vikings Play-by-Play Announcer
Signing Brett Favre, I think it's absolutely fantastic. The stars have aligned, what more can you say? Brett Favre is an iconic figure. He is a legitimate, bona fide superstar, and he plays for the Minnesota Vikings, which makes me very excited. As a player, he is just so full of exuberance and he wears his emotions on his sleeve. That is why the fans adore him. He is also a very polarizing figure, as well, which is why there are so many compelling story lines to this season. A lot of people talk about us using Brett for a new stadium and him using us to get back at Ted Thompson—for whatever the reasons, this is a torrid love affair, and I am just thrilled to be a small part of it.

As for the whole revenge thing, I am not too sure what to make of it all. I know that he and Ted had a falling out of sorts, but nobody really knows for sure why. Was it the fact that they didn't sign Randy Moss? Who knows. I gotta say this about Ted, though, he's got guts. Back when everything started to go south up there, Brett was wavering over whether or not he wanted to keep playing. Eventually, Ted had to make a decision and he went with Aaron Rodgers. I respect the fact that he eyeballed football immortality and said no. Not many people can do that in this business, and it had to be tough. I know that a lot of Green Bay fans are mad at him over that, but you've got to give him props for standing his ground....

I think Brett's number-one reason for coming here was to win a Super Bowl. He saw that we were a perfect fit and he jumped on it. Having said that, I am sure he wants to win that game up in Lambeau pretty badly. The guy is the ultimate competitor, so I am sure he had that date circled on his calendar a long time ago. What will it be like to watch Favre step foot onto Lambeau Field? In my eight years of

doing play-by-play with the Vikings, it will probably be the most sur-real moment that I have ever experienced. To watch him run out wearing purple and to hear the cascade of boos and cheers is going to be unlike anything I have ever seen before. I am sure the Green Bay fans are going to be beside themselves. Nothing would make me happier to absolutely beat the bleep out of the Packers that day, nothing. I can't wait. Ironically, my current professional highlight also came in Lambeau, back in 2004, when the Vikings beat the Pack as a seven-point underdog in the wild-card playoff game. It had a lot of significance because at the time beating Brett Favre was such an accomplishment.

> "As a player, he is just so full of exuberance and he wears his emotions on his sleeve. That is why the fans adore him."
> — Paul Allen

Ever since Brett has gotten here, the fan reaction has been through the roof. I talk to callers all day on the radio who have opinions, one way or the other, about this, and it is crazy. To the fans who hate Favre just because he was a Packer, I think that is just stupid. That provincial take is short-sighted, at best. You can't put your personal feelings in front of the big picture. I mean, if you love this team, you have to realize that this guy probably gives you the best chance to do something that you have never done—win a Super Bowl. Brett Favre, through the first five weeks of the season last year, led the NFL in passing yards. Then his arm went south. Well, we know what was wrong with his arm, and he got it fixed. So he is good to go. He gives this team its best chance to finally win a championship since 1998. So, with all due respect to those fans who are haters, *get over it!*

Mark Rosen
Longtime Twin Cities TV Sports Anchor
To see Brett Favre in purple is beyond surreal. It is something I never thought that I would see, at least in my lifetime. As a journalist, I

Brett Favre smiles on the sideline late in the game in Cleveland during the Vikings' opening-day, 34–20 victory over the Browns on September 13, 2009. *Photo courtesy of Getty Images*

couldn't be happier about this whole story. It's been huge. It's also been a wonderful diversion from the *real* problems going on out there with the economy and wars and what have you. The whole thing has been like a roller-coaster ride, with plenty of ups and downs. I will be honest, though, I was down in the dumps emotionally when he decided at first not to come right before training camp. It was a big disappointment, a real letdown. You could literally feel it down in Mankato [at training camp]. Everybody was down, the players, the coaches, the Vikings staffers, the fans, and even the media. We were all expecting fireworks, and in the end we got snubbed when he didn't show up.

Then, when it happened and he signed, everybody was just beside themselves. It was almost numbing. As a fan and journalist it was hard to separate the two that day, it was pretty emotional. To see his rock star-like arrival, with the live TV coverage and helicopter following

him around, it was unbelievable. I don't know of another athlete that could have elicited that sort of response. I think we were all so Favred-out over the past several months, it was just an "Is it really true?" kind of a moment. I will never forget it.

It was a sense of relief, too, because in my heart I just knew that this team should not be having a quarterback battle. Contending teams don't have those problems, they have a clear starter, *the* guy who can lead them to victory. Well, Brett Favre is now *the* guy in Minnesota. The fact that he wants to be here and wants to lead this team to the Super Bowl was just what the fans up here wanted and needed to hear. They have been waiting and waiting for so long, and this guy, if nothing else, represents hope. He gives us a legitimate shot, which is something we haven't had since at least 1998. The team has a real aura behind it now, a swagger, and that is just really exciting to see.

As for why he chose to come here, I think it just made sense for him. He gets the opportunity to get revenge; he steps into an offense that he is extremely comfortable with; he knows the coaching staff; he has the best running back in football lined up behind him; he has an outstanding defense that will keep him in games; he will be playing in a domed stadium; and he has a legitimate chance to get to the Super Bowl here. I would have to believe that it's the perfect fit, in his eyes. It comes with a whole bunch of controversy, though. The fact of the matter is that Brett had choices, and he chose to come here. The Green Bay fans are really upset, and deservedly so. They are burning Favre jerseys and destroying his bobble-head dolls, it's a stab to the heart as far as they are concerned. The Packers and Vikings have one of the richest rivalries in the NFL, and these two organizations do not like each other. As for the fans, they *really* don't like each other. Some of it is good-natured and fun, while some is pretty emotional. In terms of heated rivals, the only thing in recent memory that would come close to this in my eyes would be Roger Clemens going from the Red Sox to the Yankees. But I think this is a *much* bigger deal, I really do.

That game up in Lambeau is going to be something special. I honestly don't know if there has ever been anything like it in sports,

certainly not in the NFL, at least that I can think of. The raw emotions of the fans up there are going to be off the charts. There are so many Favre fans in Wisconsin who are so deeply hurt by this and are just beside themselves. I have never seen anything like it. They have been cheering for this guy since day one, and now he is playing for their bitter enemy. Now they have to root against him and hope he falls on his face. You just can't make this stuff up. It's priceless.

The bottom line in my mind is that this team needed a quarterback who can win in January, when it counts—and that is what they got in Brett Favre. I don't know where we are at with regards to a new stadium for this team, but if Brett Favre ends up hoisting the Lombardi Trophy over his head come February in Miami, I would have to think

> *"They have been cheering for this guy since day one, and now he is playing for their bitter enemy. Now they have to root against him and hope he falls on his face. You just can' t make this stuff up. It's priceless."*
> —*Mark Rosen*

our chances would markedly improve. Let's hope on both accounts. It's going to be one heck of a season, that's for sure.

Tim Yotter
Publisher of Viking Update *Magazine*
We have been tracking this story for over a year, obviously, and it has been a roller coaster. When rumors would heat up, our Web hits would spike, and it would get really crazy. Then things would die down, only to get heated up again by some blog report of this or that. It was complete Favre overload. We would have four Favre-related stories on our website and all of them would get a ton of hits. It was unlike anything we had ever seen before. Not even close.

I have always enjoyed watching Brett Favre play. Beyond the records and all of that, he is just an extremely entertaining player. The way he plays, with such passion, is wonderful. I have never seen

another quarterback in all my years who has displayed that type of enthusiasm. Most quarterbacks are low-key, cerebral, and almost robot-like. Favre is the polar opposite of that, and I think that is why so many fans from so many walks of life admire him. When you watch him play, you almost feel like he is just as much a fan as he is a player out there, because of how excited he gets.

> "Brett Favre sells tickets and creates interest. He also wins games. Lots of games. Could you imagine if he led this team to its first Super Bowl title? This town would go crazy."
> —Rod Simons

I give Zygi Wilf a lot of credit for making this all happen. I think that gets lost a little bit in this story. I mean that guy wants to win so badly and has been willing to do just about whatever it takes to bring this team a Super Bowl. You have to respect that, you really do. He put his money where his mouth was when it came to shelling out $25 million to get Brett, and I think the fans should be really thankful for that. Hopefully, this team will have great success, and he will be rewarded down the road with a new stadium. Let's all keep our fingers crossed.

Rod Simons
Twin Cities TV Sports Anchor
The whole thing is beyond surreal. I live in a house divided right now. For me, I am thrilled. As a fan, I couldn't be more excited about our chances. To see No. 4 running this offense is just what the doctor ordered, in my book. My wife, on the other hand, thinks the guy is just a complete drama queen, and she is repulsed by his narcissistic attitude. That is Brett Favre to a tee—completely polarizing. And it is like that all over, which I think is utterly fascinating. The fans are divided up here, they either love him or hate him—it's like there is no gray area with him.

His signing goes way beyond wins and losses, too. Brett Favre is big business. He certainly affected my business in a positive way, that's for sure. In fact, he put my show *Sports Final* back on the air, literally. A month before Brett signed we were gasping for air, looking for advertising and sponsorship. I wasn't sure if we were going to get it done, to be honest, which would have meant that we would have gotten canceled. Then, once the rumors heated up and the helicopters came out, it was like a light switch went on. Everybody started calling, and we were back in business just like that. It was amazing. I can directly attribute it to his signing, without a doubt.

Take it to the next level, and you can see why signing him was a brilliant move by the team's ownership group. Brett Favre sells tickets and creates interest. He also wins games. Lots of games. Could you imagine if he led this team to its first Super Bowl title? This town would go crazy....

As for why Brett chose to come to Minnesota, Green Bay's biggest rival? I think the guy just wants to play. I don't buy the whole revenge thing, either. The guy has made too much money and had too much success to have held a grudge for this long, considering the success that they had in Green Bay for all those years. I hear the conspiracy theorists, but I don't see it. I think he sees the best running back in the league in Adrian Peterson, a stable of pretty good receivers, a decent offensive line, and a solid defense that will keep the other team out of the end zone. The Vikings have a very good football team, but the one piece of the puzzle that had been lacking was a dynamic quarterback. He is that piece.

Plus, this is it for Brett, and he knows it. This is his last best chance to win a Super Bowl and to go out on top. I also think that Giants playoff game a couple of years ago still haunts him, and he wants to make up for it. So, for all those reasons, I think that's why he is a Minnesota Viking—not for revenge. The guy is a legend. He doesn't need to get any revenge. I just hope he has enough gas left in the tank to finish the season and take us to the promised land. Lord knows, there is a lot riding on it.

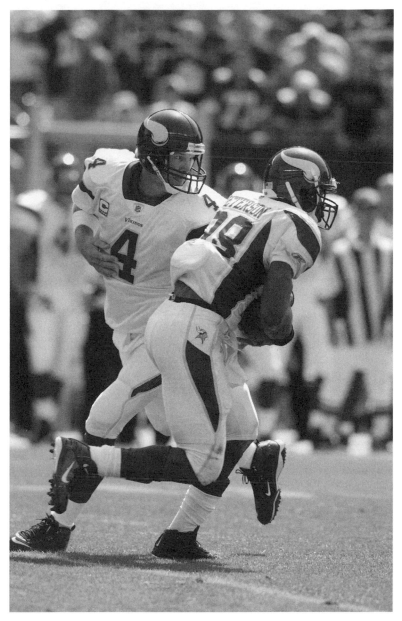

Brett Favre hands off to Vikings running back Adrian Peterson during Favre's regular-season debut against the Cleveland Browns on September 13, 2009.

Sean Jensen
Vikings Beat Writer for the Pioneer Press

I covered the Packers for the *Milwaukee Journal Sentinel* in 1998 and got to spend a season with [Favre] in Green Bay. That was the year after they won the Super Bowl, and it was quite an experience. Brett was like a god up there, no question. He pretty much owned that town. Despite all of that, he was very approachable and he seemed like a pretty down-to-earth kind of a guy. I mean, he would show up every day in ratty shorts, an old T-shirt, and flip flops. So, 12 years later, I never thought in my wildest dreams that I would now be covering him as a Minnesota Viking. It's pretty surreal.

As for how his signing has effected me as a journalist, it's been crazy. The speculation and rumors leading up to it was just exhausting, to be honest. Then, when the story finally broke, it was just a blur. The fans are extremely interested, though, and I would guess that at least 75 percent of all my stories since he signed have included his name in it. I feel terrible about that in some regards, too, because this team has a potential No. 1 defense, and I haven't really written about them at all. Even for defensive-related stories, I have found myself asking the players about Favre. There is just never a shortage of stories related to the guy, whether that's breaking news or rumors or what have you. And, frankly, there is no shortage of demand for those stories. Every story I write that is related to him ends up being one of the most popular stories on our website. It's funny, but I keep thinking I just can't write any more about the guy, but then I always come up with something else, another angle. It's wild, it really is. Long, long hours and lots of digging. It has been exciting. I have been doing a lot of TV interviews on ESPN, talking about Brett, which is fun, too.

The interest in Favre just ramps up everything for everyone. It has had a positive effect on a lot of things, too, from media coverage to ticket sales to just the overall atmosphere in the community. People here are just really excited about this team and about its chances this year. Overall, Minnesota fans have really embraced him. In his first two weeks with the team, Favre's No. 4 jersey sold more than any

other NFL player's had in all of 2009, surpassing Jay Cutler's, which fell to second on the list. That just shows you how popular the guy is. If he can somehow lead this team to its first-ever Super Bowl championship, the level of excitement is going to be off the charts—like nothing we have ever seen here. There is a lot riding on his shoulders right now, from Childress' job to the owner's desire to get a new stadium built downtown. To borrow the poker term, by signing Brett Favre, these guys are all-in. They are just hoping to ride this momentum as far as they can, absolutely.

> "People here are just really excited about this team and about its chances this year. Overall, Minnesota fans have really embraced him. In his first two weeks with the team, Favre's No. 4 jersey sold more than any other NFL player's had in all of 2009."
> —Sean Jensen

As for why Brett ultimately wound up in Minnesota, I hate to put myself into somebody else's head, but it's pretty evident that he's not the most decisive person. Obviously, even before last year, he put the Packers through a lot of drama a couple of times during the off-season about not being sure if he wanted to return. Last year they called him on his bluff to retire and decided that they were finally going to move on. Then, by the time he changed his mind, they dug their heels into the ground and said, "Hey, we're moving forward, as we told you we would." I'm sure there's an element of him that felt sort of betrayed by that just because he's done so much for that franchise. I would imagine he wants to prove to those guys that he's still a good quarterback in this league to prove them wrong. So, yes, I do think that there was an element of revenge in his decision to come to Minnesota, but I don't think it's one of the top three reasons he decided to ultimately sign here. I really don't. For the most part, he knew that the Vikings were a team that needed a quarterback, and he knew that many of the pieces were already in place here. I think that's the bottom line.

Bob Sansevere
Longtime Sports Columnist for the Pioneer Press

The whole story has been just fascinating. I have never seen anything like it in all my years, that's for sure. I mean, the tone was set right out of the gates when Brett referred to Brad Childress as "Chilly" at his opening press conference. I asked around to some of the other players and coaches, and none of them would even dare call him that, which I thought was pretty interesting. Those two are friends and obviously have a history together, and it just adds a really compelling dynamic to it all. How that relationship plays out this season will be the big story, in my eyes. People are just extremely curious about Brett Favre, both here as well as nationally. I mean, look at that Monday night preseason game he started against Houston—ESPN's ratings were at an all-time high for it. That says a lot.

I think what Brett Favre gives this team is an element of fear. His presence makes opposing defenses respect what the Vikings can do offensively. Teams have to respect what Favre is capable of doing, especially when it comes to passing the ball downfield. That is something this team simply did not have with Tarvaris Jackson or Sage Rosenfels. He also gives this team an element of hope, which is something they desperately need. Optimism is running high around here, and that is great to see. Expectations are also running high, so we will have to see how this season plays out. On paper this team looks really good, so if Favre can be that missing piece, then this will turn out to be an excellent investment.

As far as the whole theory of Favre coming here to help get the owner a new stadium, I am not sure if I totally buy into that. Yes, it would certainly help, but there are no guarantees. I think that this team is eventually going to have to start signing some one-year leases at the Metrodome until they can figure out a long-term solution. In this economy, I just don't see a whole lot of momentum by the legislature with regards to appropriating funds to this. On the other hand, I can't imagine this team moving to Los Angeles, either. I mean, California has probably been hit harder than any other state

economy-wise, and I have a hard time believing that anyone would even consider building a new stadium without a team right now. I know that there are some big wheels in that group of investors out there, but I think everybody is having money problems right now. We'll just have to wait and see.

I don't buy into the whole revenge thing, either. I really don't. I think it was more about him wanting to come to a team that was a good fit and that had a reasonable chance to go to a Super Bowl. He has that here, plain and simple. I mean, he is playing in front of the best running back in the game on a team that has one of the best defenses in football. It's a good situation for him, no question. It's been good for us in the media, too, because there are never a shortage of interesting angles and storylines to follow in all of this. It's going to be a fun season.

Fans Love Brett Favre

Syd Davy
Vikings Super Fan Who Dresses Up as the Character
"100% Cheese Free"

I am a die-hard Minnesota Vikings fan, no doubt about it. I bleed purple. I drive nearly eight hours each way for every home game from Winnipeg, up in Canada. That is how much I love the purple. Last year I won "Tailgater of the Year in the NFL," and I even started a fan group called the "Viking World Order," which has over 1,200 members. Membership requires getting a tattoo, so we are all pretty committed to the cause. I was the big guy with the purple face paint who caught Randy Moss in the end zone for all those years. How much fun was that? He even invited me out to New England to catch him last year for a Monday night game, it was pretty neat. Now I catch Adrian Peterson, which is pretty neat, too. I live for the Vikes, man, this team and these players are my life.

So what do I think about my team getting Brett Favre? I love it. I think Favre coming to Minnesota is great. Congratulations, Brett, you are now officially 100 percent cheese free! He finally got that horrible stench of moldy cheese off of him, and we are thrilled to have him

Recently converted Brett Favre fans show their new quarterback some love at a 2009 preseason game against the Kansas City Chiefs in the Metrodome.

here. Hopefully he will help us finally win a Super Bowl, that is all I really care about. Now, there are a lot of Minnesota fans who absolutely hate Brett Favre. But they want a Super Bowl so badly that they are willing to put up with him. At the end of the day, that is what it is really all about. I mean, if we win a championship with Favre, I

would have to think it would be a done deal to get a new stadium. You couldn't possibly let a championship team move to Los Angeles, could you? I sure hope not, and so do all the other Vikings fans out there. Look, if there is one thing I want before I die, it is to watch the Vikings finally win a Super Bowl. I go to the big game every year, and it sucks to see all the other teams in it all the time.

In 2004 I was made an honorary captain for the Vikings-versus-Packers game, and I got to meet Favre on the field for the coin toss at the start of the game. He reached over to shake my hand, and I grabbed it and squeezed as hard as I could—and I am a pretty big guy. I leaned over and said, "We're gonna kick your ass!" He just smiled and said, "We'll see about that!" He is a tough guy, and I am just glad that he is finally playing with us, instead of

> *"Congratulations, Brett, you are now officially 100 percent cheese free!"*
> *—Syd Davy*

against us. I like our chances this year with old No. 4 back there, absolutely. Maybe this is our year? It is our time, it really is. A good quarterback has always been the missing piece to this puzzle, and now that we have that, watch out! Go Vikings!

Mike Nowakowski
Owner of Ticket King

We have offices in both the Twin Cities and Green Bay, so we have certainly reaped the benefits of having Brett Favre around for the last 17 years. The bottom line with regards to tickets is that Brett Favre made that product for Green Bay. Twenty years ago, Packer tickets were not a big deal. I mean, nobody was going to spend big money to see Don Majkowski. Once Favre got there, though, everything changed. Prior to Favre, maybe you would see the top seats go for $100, whereas after he got there, those same seats might go for as much as $500. He had that kind of impact. People were willing to pay big bucks to see him play. He is the real deal. Very few athletes have

that quality, and he is certainly one of them. We have seen a huge run on tickets since Brett signed with the Vikings, and that is no coincidence. Needless to say, our Minneapolis office has benefited immensely. The week he signed, we had our best week revenue-wise ever, and we have been in business for over 20 years. Look, he is arguably the best quarterback to ever play the game, and fans on both sides of the border want to see him play. Period.

> *"I have felt the anguish that the Vikings fans have felt over the past couple of decades, and Brett Favre has given them hope."*
> —Mike Nowakowski

As for me, personally, I was born and raised in Wisconsin, but now I live in Minnesota, so I understand just how big the rivalry really is. My business is directly tied to the Vikings as well as the Packers, however, so now I root for them both to do well. However well those teams do is the difference between my family eating steak or Spam for dinner. That is just the way it goes. I have felt the anguish that the Vikings fans have felt over the past couple of decades, and Brett Favre has given them hope. He has put the team on the front page of the national media, and that is a good thing.

In my opinion, whether you were the biggest Vikings fan in the world or just a casual fan, you can't really hate the guy. Fans really enjoy watching him, regardless of their allegiance. The guy is just a tough competitor, and you have to respect that. Deep down, I really admire the guy. In fact, I even gave my wife the okay to date him years ago, to put him on her "list." You know, where you each get to have one person outside of your marriage. Now that he's moved to the Twin Cities, though, I may have to ask my wife to revise her list!

Betty Custer
Wisconsin Native and Die-Hard Brett Favre Fan
I feel very badly about him playing for the Vikings, I really do. I am a die-hard Packers fan and I just hate the Vikings. I hate them even

At his home debut in the Metrodome on September 27, 2009, Vikings fans learned what it means to love Brett Favre. With two seconds left in the game, he connected with wide receiver Greg Lewis on a 32-yard TD pass, completing the Vikings' 27–24 come-from-behind victory over the San Francisco 49ers.

more so than the Bears, which means I *really* hate the Vikings! So to see Brett wearing purple is so difficult. The whole thing is just terrible, just awful. But I am a rabid Brett Favre fan, and I will *always* love him. Always. And even though he now plays for the enemy, I will always cheer for him to do well—just as long as it is not against the Packers.

I will never stop cheering for him, never. I will continue to wear my Favre Green Bay jersey, too, absolutely. People around here think I am crazy to say that, but that is just how I feel. I could never boo him, either, no way. So many people are so mad at him for what he did, feeling like he is a diva now and that he has changed, but I still love him. Call me bipolar, schizophrenic, or whatever, I just can't let go. I will always root for him, regardless of where he plays.

I have been rooting for this team for many, many years, going back to Paul Hornung and Bart Starr. Never, however, have I seen a player who played with more passion than Brett. You just watch him and you can see that he totally enjoys being out there on the field. His love of the game is contagious, it really is. He is just a normal person. Sure, he is a multimillionaire many times over and world famous, but he makes us feel like he is just like the rest of us. That is a pretty neat thing to be able to do, to be so successful yet still be able to make people feel like you aren't any better than they are.

> "I am a rabid Brett Favre fan, and I will always love him. Always. And even though he now plays for the enemy, I will always cheer for him to do well—just as long as it is not against the Packers."
>
> —Betty Custer

I am a coach's daughter, so I understand the passion that some people have for sports. Brett can't let go and he really just wants to play. I understand that. I wish it was for any other team besides the Vikings, but it is what it is, I suppose.... I will be honest, though, I think the Packers did him wrong. I was *very* upset with the organization last year when they traded him to the Jets. Very upset. I think that Ted Thompson should have treated him with more respect. He deserved it, in my opinion. I know that Brett is bitter about that, and that is probably why he chose to play in Minnesota. Who knows? I am still a Packers fan, though, and always will be. I have been a Packers fan much longer than I have been a Brett fan, so that will continue for

as long as I live. And, as much as it pains me to say it, if Brett was able to win another Super Bowl before he retired, I would genuinely be happy for him—even though that would mean Minnesota would finally be winning a championship. Oh, my gosh, what am I saying? Maybe I really am schizophrenic!

SOURCES

Introduction: Why I Love Brett Favre

BRETT FAVRE'S TOP 10 CAREER MOMENTS: ESPN Research August 19, 2009 (http://sports.espn.go.com/nfl/news/story?id=3276455).

Players Love Brett Favre

STEVE MARIUCCI: "Mariucci Has Faith in Favre's Ability," by Sid Hartman, *Star Tribune*, August 20, 2009.

JON GRUDEN: "Gruden Calls Favre Perfect Fit for Vikings," by Sid Hartman, *Star Tribune*, August 30, 2009.

FRANK WINTERS: *Favre: The Man/The Legend* (CD), by the Milwaukee Journal Sentinel, Triumph Books, Chicago, IL, 2008.

DOUG PEDERSON: *Favre: The Man/The Legend* (CD), by the Milwaukee Journal Sentinel, Triumph Books, Chicago, IL, 2008.

DARRELL BEVELL: "Bevell's High Opinion of Favre Now Higher," by Sid Hartman, *Star Tribune*, August 28, 2009.

The Media Love Brett Favre

DON BANKS: "Favre to Vikings," by Don Banks, SI.com, August 18, 2009.

SETH WICKERSHAM: "Don't Fault Favre for Returning," by Seth Wickersham, *ESPN The Magazine*, August 19, 2009.

Brett Favre (left) celebrates after throwing a 54-yard touchdown pass to Andre Rison during the first quarter of the Packers' Super Bowl XXXI victory over the New England Patriots in New Orleans on January 26, 1997. Favre (above) hugs offensive lineman Aaron Taylor after another TD later in the same game.

In one of the most memorable performances of his career, on December 22, 2003, Favre played a *Monday Night Football* game the day after his father Irv died and threw for 399 yards and four touchdowns in a blowout 41–7 victory over the Oakland Raiders. *Photo courtesy of Getty Images*